The Seer Advantage

The Seer Advantage

A BIBLICAL MODEL

TO DREAMS & VISIONS

INTERPRETATION

Tamara McNair-Hicks, JD

THE SEER ADVANTAGE by Tamara McNair-Hicks, JD
Published by RainFire Ministries
8707 Hollow Creek Circle
Charlotte, NC 28262
www.rainfireministries.org
info@rainfireministries.org

This book or parts thereof may not be reproduced in any form, stored in a retrieval system, or transmitted in any form by any means— electronic, mechanical, photocopy, recording, or otherwise—without prior written permission of the publisher, except as provided by United States of America copyright law.

Unless otherwise noted, all Scripture quotations are from the Holy Bible, English Standard Version. Copyright © 2001 by Crossway Bibles, a division of Good News Publishers. Used by permission.

Scripture quotations marked AMP are from the Amplified Bible. Copyright © 2015 by The Lockman Foundation, La Habra, CA 90631. All rights reserved. Used by permission.

Scripture quotations marked AMPC are from the Amplified Bible, Classic Edition. Copyright © 1954, 1958, 1962, 1964, 1965, 1987 by The Lockman Foundation. Used by permission.

Scripture quotations marked KJV are from the King James Version of the Bible.

Scripture quotations marked NASB are from the New American Standard Bible, copyright © 1960, 1962, 1963, 1968, 1971, 1972, 1973, 1975, 1977, 1995 by The Lockman Foundation. Used by permission. (www.Lockman.org)

Scripture quotations marked NIV are taken from the Holy Bible, New International Version®, NIV®. Copyright © 1973, 1978, 1984, 2011 by Biblica, Inc.™ Used by permission of Zondervan. All rights reserved worldwide. www.zondervan.com. The "NIV" and "New International Version" are trademarks registered in the United States Patent and Trademark Office by Biblica, Inc.™

Scripture quotations marked NKJV are taken from the New King James Version®. Copyright © 1982 by Thomas Nelson. Used by permission. All rights reserved.

Scripture quotations marked NLT are from the Holy Bible, New Living Translation, copyright © 1996, 2004, 2007. Used by permission of Tyndale House Publishers, Inc., Wheaton, IL 60189. All rights reserved.

Copyright © 2018 by Tamara McNair-Hicks
All rights reserved

Visit the author's website at www.rainfireministries.org.
International Standard Book Number: 978-1-71890-671-6
ISBN-10: 1718906714

While the author has made every effort to provide accurate internet addresses at the time of publication, neither the publisher nor the author assumes any responsibility for errors or for changes that occur after publication. Further, the publisher does not have any control over and does not assume any responsibility for author or third-party websites or their content.

18 19 20 21 22 — 987654321
Printed in the United States of America

*To all the seers who have been looking for their place
in the body of Christ*

To my family who prayed this book into existence

To my friends, both new and old, who believed in me

CONTENTS

Foreword by John Eckhardt xi

Introduction
    Welcome to the Dreamer's Realm.................. xiii

Chapter One
    What Makes the Seer and the Prophet Different? 1

Chapter Two
    Characteristics of the Seer.......................... 9

Chapter Three
    Demystifying Dreams and Visions 21

Chapter Four
    How the Seer Gift Positions You 31

Chapter Five
    How We Lost the Ability to See 41

Chapter Six
    A Good Character 49

Chapter Seven
    Holy Spirit—the Seer's Guide 57

Chapter Eight
    A Prophet, Not a Psychic......................... 61

Chapter Nine

    Realms of the Spirit 77

Chapter Ten

    How to Respond to Your Dreams and Visions 87

Conclusion

    Embrace Your Seer Gift 93

Appendix A

    References to Dreams in Scripture 97

Appendix B

    Symbolic Numbers and Colors in Dreams 103

Notes 105

FOREWORD

I WANT TO PERSONALLY recommend and endorse *The Seer Advantage* by Tamara McNair-Hicks, JD. This new book on dreams will give you insight and revelation that will change your life. Tamara has pressed into the dream realm for many years. Her prayer life, biblical studies, and obedience to God have given her supernatural insight into the seer realm.

In this book, you will be challenged to understand your dreams and the dreams of others. The seer realm is real and amazing. At times, however, it can be difficult for many to understand. It takes supernatural wisdom from the Holy Spirit to comprehend dreams properly.

I have known Tamara for several years, and I am amazed at the wisdom she possesses in this area. I love her willingness and desire to impart this wisdom to others. She has a passion to see the body of Christ rise and move into this realm.

God has always used dreams to communicate with His people. Dreams break the limitations of the natural mind and help us to connect with the spirit realm. God is using dreams today to unlock mysteries from heaven. Understanding your dreams will give you an advantage in life. God has a plan and purpose for your life that can only be discerned spiritually; you have in your hands a book that will help you walk in destiny and purpose.

The dream realm is also very symbolic. There are many symbols in the Bible that need to be understood that will help you better comprehend your dreams. It is important to have a solid biblical basis for proper dream interpretation.

I would not recommend all books on dreams. There are many

New Age teachings on dreams that can lead you astray. I know Tamara's life and her commitment to the Word of God. Her foundation in the Lord is strong, and her teaching on dreams is biblically sound.

I pray that as you read this book, God will give you understanding in all things. This book will challenge you and stretch you. Don't be afraid to launch out into the deep. Don't be afraid to live a supernatural lifestyle. I believe many breakthroughs will happen in your life as you understand the seer realm. Get ready to increase in wisdom and understanding as you read *The Seer Advantage*.

—APOSTLE JOHN ECKHARDT
OVERSEER, CRUSADERS MINISTRIES
BEST-SELLING AUTHOR, *PRAYERS THAT ROUT DEMONS*
CHICAGO, IL

Introduction

WELCOME TO THE DREAMER'S REALM

FROM AS FAR back as I can remember, I have been able to see into the spirit through dreams and visions but also with my natural eyes, which initially caused great confusion and fear. There was very little information about being a prophet and even less about the visionary realm when I was growing up in the Lord. I was truly taught by the Holy Spirit, He led me and guided me to understanding my gift. It wasn't until sometime later that I even realized conversations with God on a regular basis are not the norm for everyone. Experiencing different responses from others regarding my gift, I started to feel different and out of place. Still I am grateful for the journey over a period of years that has led me to the understanding I have today.

One of the first things we need to understand is that the significance and impact of dreams are not limited by the age of the dreamer. The earliest dream I remember having happened when I was seven. I will never forget this dream. It was about my immediate family, which consisted of four people—my mother, father, sister, and me. I love my family and had such a great childhood. My mother attended church and made sure that my sister and I attended regularly as well, but my father had yet to give his life to Christ.

In this dream, all four of us were standing on a grid of some sort. It was red with big circles that each of us stood in. Suddenly,

I looked up and saw angels dressed in white and gold descending from the sky. They grabbed hold of my mother's hand and took her up toward the sky. As she ascended, my mother caught my sister by the hand. Then my sister reached down and took my hand. When I reached for my father's hand, I missed it. I couldn't grab hold of it as I rose up into the sky. Left behind, he sat down and begin to sink into the red grid. It was as if he was going into the abyss of hell.

Though I was very young when I had this dream, I understood very well what it meant. It scared me to the point that, even at seven years old, I began to pray for my father's salvation. And I prayed until the day he accepted Christ some years later. This was the dream that marked the beginning of my affair with dreams and visions.

THE DREAMER'S ADVANTAGE

There is an advantage to walking closely with God. He shares His secrets with those who walk closely with Him (Amos 3:7). He "confides in those who fear Him" (Ps. 25:14, NIV). God uses the nighttime to release dreams and visions that impart great revelations and speak great truths to us. Job 33:15–16 says,

> In a dream, in a vision of the night, when deep sleep falls upon men, while slumbering on their beds, then He opens the ears of men, and seals their instruction.

The enemy continues to try to bring fear to the nighttime and the dream realm. He wants to keep us away from its power and advantages, and to shield our true operation in the kingdom of God. Through TV and movies such as *Nightmare on Elm Street* and Stephen King's *It*, this realm has been taken over by Satan, and we are now at a disadvantage. The nighttime has been demonized, and we have been indoctrinated to believe that the night belongs to the demonic world, but it doesn't. Both the day and the night belong to the Lord (Ps. 74:16).

Throughout this book, we will explore how to avoid the traps set in place to detour us from recognizing our true potential. From dream and vision interpretation to understanding the mysteries of heaven, we will open up the seer realm in a practical and biblical way to make it easily accessible to all believers who are willing to be activated into this realm. We will also explore how you can maneuver within this realm, thus gaining the advantage you were meant to possess.

SEEING VS. HEARING

There are a lot of different teachings out there about the seer and the prophet. One prevalent teaching in the church is that there is no difference between the seer and the prophet. I personally believe, however, that there is a difference between the two, and I will show you how to use both to build one upon the other, increasing the effectiveness of your gift.

Because I have always been a seer (one who understands God visually), it was difficult at first to understand the ways of a *nabiy* prophet or a prophet who hears God's voice then has the unction to prophesy and speak forth the word of the Lord (also called a bubbling up or bubbling forth).[1] My prophetic education with the Holy Spirit allowed me to transition from the visual realm to the hearing dimension over a period of time. I now understand that there are levels to be attained in the prophetic and that they build on one another. This transition was eye opening form me and it paved the way for me to begin to understand the importance of melding the two worlds together. Prophets who only see visions or dream dreams may find it hard to comprehend the two streams, but there needs to be an appreciation and understanding for both diversities.

When I was first trying to understand my gift, as compared

to other's who hear, I was confused a lot. I would see a vision or a picture, but I did not hear actual words and I did not have the adequate language to explain what I saw. I thought perhaps I wasn't a prophet, because I did not operate the way other hearing prophets did. Over time and through a series of biblical steps, the Lord showed me otherwise.

Are You a Dreamer?

Everyone who has a dream or vision is not automatically a prophet. So, you may be asking, "How do I know if I'm a prophet?" There is a protocol that the Bible sets in place for the prophetic office. I will share this simple, three-part biblical process with you now.

1. Have you been called in a dream?

The Scriptures tell us in Numbers 12:6 that you can be called in a dream:

> And He said, Hear now my words: If there be a prophet among you, I the Lord will make myself known unto him in a vision, and will speak unto him in a dream.
>
> —KJV

This was actually the first way I was called as a prophet by the Lord.

2. Have you been called through Scripture?

The second way He called me was through a more formal means, which was through Scripture. Jeremiah 1:5 was one of the main verses He used to confirm His calling, though there are others. It reads:

> Before I formed you in the womb I knew you, before you born I set you apart; I appointed you as a prophet to the nations.
>
> —NIV

The Lord used this exact scripture to speak to me about who I was destined to be. At the time, I wasn't aware what a prophet is, so it took some time for me to grasp this part of my confirmation.

3. Have you been confirmed by other prophets?

Lastly, you can be confirmed as a prophet by other mature prophets or presbytery.

I remember sitting in church one day when a guest prophet came to speak and minister to us. In the middle of their preaching, they stopped, looked at me, pointed, and said, "The reason you have all the dreams and visions you have is because you are a true prophet of God."

That was only one of the four times God allowed me to have this experience. Being confirmed in this way is a demonstration of another scripture that says, "By the mouth of two or three witnesses every word shall be established" (1 Cor. 13:1).

As you grow in the realm of prophecy through hearing God's voice and by seeing dreams and visions, the Lord will also confirm this gift in you. He will teach you how to operate in this gift so that you will be an effective member of His body. He will also send resources and mature prophets to assist you on your journey. This book is one of those resources, and my journey is one that you can learn from.

So, if you have ever felt strange or out of place, as I did, and if you desire to understand the gift God has given you, I am writing this book for you. It is my hope that, as I share my journey with you, the feeling of being cursed or different will be erased and you will know the truth that you are called out and unique.

Chapter One

WHAT MAKES THE SEER AND THE PROPHET DIFFERENT?

WHAT IS THE seer realm? According his book *The Seer*, James Goll defines the realm in this way:

> Within the overall realm of the prophet lies the particular and distinctive realm of *the seer*. The word *seer* describes a particular type of prophet who receives a particular type of prophetic revelation or impartation. The word *seer* was used in the Old Testament prior to the use of the word *prophet*.[1]

The Bible states in Amos 3:7:

> For the Lord God does nothing without revealing his secret to his servants the prophets.

Unfortunately, when we think of the ways in which Jehovah reveals Himself we typically, imagine the *nabiy* prophet. We have a very clear example of this prophet in church. In most pulpits today, there is wide spread teaching on the prophetic. It takes the form of words of knowledge, words of wisdom, and prophecy. We are given many examples of these types of prophets.

The church has neglected the realm of the seer or the prophet who works in the visual realm. We tend to think differently about those whose main function involves this gift. Prophets such as Daniel, Ezekiel, Joseph, and Asaph are often marginalized into categories that do not show their depth within this supernatural realm. They had great visions and dreams and dealt with angels and demons. If we look further, their supernatural encounters put them in direct contact with God on a greater level. Yet somehow, we have missed or dismissed our need for this insight in the church.

There are different streams of the prophetic office. Within in the context of Scripture, there are varying Hebrew words used to describe the prophet. These words will give us a different description of the types of prophets we encounter. There are *nabiy*, *ra'ah*, *chozeh*, and *ro'eh* prophets. You will find the context for this passage in 1 Chronicles 29:29, which reads:

> Now the acts of King David, from first to last are written in the chronicles of Samuel the seer [*ra'ah*], in the chronicles of Nathan the prophet [*nabiy*] and in the chronicles of Gad the seer [*chozeh*].[2]

These Hebrew words are vital to how we encounter and understand the prophetic. A *ra'ah* prophet will have the senses to see or to have visions. *Ra'ah* can also mean "to look at" or "to gaze."[3] This prophet has actual visions that can seem so real as though they can reach out and touch the images they see. They can also operate in a category of open visions or open heavens.

The *chozeh* prophet is a "beholder in vision."[4] It also means a prophet who sees within their mind and does not necessarily have open visions, where the objects or images seem to be physically available in the external world. These seers experience visions that they picture in their minds. Let me give an example: even though I'm not physically holding a baseball, I can picture what a baseball looks like. I don't physically have one in my hand, but, in my mind, I can picture it.

Ro'eh, another word for "seer," is just like a *chozeh* prophet. They can have visions through trances, dreams, or images in their minds. This shows that there are different seers have different levels of sight within the prophetic realm.

The *nabiy* prophet is the prophet who hears God. His ear is attuned to heaven and when the word comes through inspiration or it bubbles forth. *Nabiy* prophets are usually the prophet for the people. They are greatly inspired by God to edify the people. The strongest aspect of their gift is receiving a word from God through hearing His voice. If a *nabiy* prophet is in a church service when the Spirit of the Lord is high, they will hear God's word and speak it forth.

This is the prophet we see operating most of the time in church. I remember feeling very confused when I was growing up, because I had a seer prophetic gift and didn't see a lot of prophets with gifts like mine. Though the Lord told me I was a prophet, there were few prophetic types beyond *nabiy* prophets that I could relate to.

Most of us will see the prophets who operate heavily in words of knowledge and wisdom. They can tell you your address, phone number, and sometimes your full name. They can lay hands on you and tell you different things that the Lord is speaking to them about you such as information about your childhood and what God is trying to do in your life. But the seer prophet will use descriptive language to reveal the word they received from the Lord about. They often use phrases such as "I *see* this" or "God is showing me that." A seer is constantly trying to decipher the unseen realm as God unfolds it to them. I like to say that the seer receives the prophetic messages of God through a movie lens. This gives us a small picture of the diversity of gifts within the seer realm.

When I first begin to understand my gift, everything I received from God was translated to me through visions and dreams. I would get vivid pictures, dreams, visions, and some trances. This was the way God spoke to me. I didn't understand how to translate them into a prophetic word. The Holy Spirit literally had to teach me the art of interpretation. All around me I witnessed *nabiy* prophets getting words from God and saying things such as, "The Lord said, 'Money will come to you tomorrow.'" However I wouldn't get a verbal word. Instead, I would just see a person standing on a stack of money, for example. Though I began to understand the meaning of the visions, I was still stuck on the fact that I did not audibly hear the words.

Eventually, I could hear a few words here and there, and as I progressed in my walk with God, I went from hearing Him sporadically to hearing Him speak to me in sentences.

THE ARRIVAL OF THE SEER

When did the seer actually arrive? The Bible says that the heavens was shut up there was no word from heaven. There were no dreams or visions, and no words were being spoken. First Samuel 1:3 is the first time we are introduced to Samuel. The Lord called him to be a prophet, and Samuel had a vision of Eli the priest. This was the first time since the heavens were closed that there was a vision from heaven.

We see, in this Bible reference, that God opened up the visionary realm. Why did God allow him to have a vision? There is a greater purpose than to deal with Eli and his sons. The Bible tells us that Samuel was the prophet who would anoint the person who would become king. Originally, judges ruled over Israel, but the people cried out to God to give them a king. Think about it this way: with a king ruling over Israel, they would be like other kingdoms. Other kingdoms had soothsayers, diviners, witchcraft, and paganism. What was God's answer to that? Raise up seers who would have the Spirit of God in them. They would be the answer to the idolatry that was prevalent in that day. With a king ruling over them, Israel was a monarch like the other kingdoms of that day which also made them subject to other laws. Because God is sovereign, He knew that they would need an advantage and so as they moved to a new type of leadership He birthed the seer realm in their midst. Bringing forth real and true prophets, He raised their ability to see into the supernatural realm to a higher degree. Seeing and operating on a new level, these prophets would be able to not only see in the now but also into the future.

Even in our times, we are seeing that God is raising up seers who can understand dreams, visions, and mysteries. He is raising them up, and they are coming on the scene. This is why I get upset when I hear people say that psychics are more accurate than prophets. I have a real problem with that. Why do I have a problem with that? The Bible doesn't tell you that. There is nowhere in the Bible to back up that statement. Why do I say that? In Daniel chapter 2, King Nebuchadnezzar had a dream and he called for all his magicians, conjurers, and sorcerers. He asked them to tell him what he dreamed and the interpretation. What did they say? "Tell the dream to your servants, and we will declare the interpretation" (v. 4, NASB). Nebuchadnezzar refused to tell them, because he knew that they would lie to him. The king understood there was a lying spirit within the diviners and that they had come together to tell him what he wanted to hear, but he wanted the truth. False teachers can give you information but not true revelation. They proceeded to tell him that "the thing which the king demands is difficult, and there is no one else who could declare it to the king except gods, whose dwelling place is not with mortal flesh" (v. 11, NASB).

Daniel, however, prayed to God, and in a night vision the mystery was made known to him. This is a testament to the power of our God. True revelation and the ability to decipher mysteries resides solely in the Holy Spirit who reveals the deep things of God. Those who reside outside of the household of faith cannot have greater understanding than the person who has the true light of God's Spirit within them. Nothing is greater than the Spirit of the living God.

When King Nebuchadnezzar saw that they could neither tell him his dream nor interpret it, he put out a decree to kill all the wise men. But Daniel, having the Spirit of God in Him, was able to tell him what he dreamed and give the interpretation, and he was right.

If you want to get revelation on things yet to be revealed in the natural, you have to have the true and living God residing inside of you. I mentioned before there are certain levels in the prophetic realm that God does not give to everyone. Not everyone is going to pay the price to get the revelation. Diviners are not better at prophecy, neither are they more adept at it than prophets. There may be times that we don't get into the presence of God like we are required, but this has no bearing on the greater authority of Jesus Christ. It is always stronger than darkness.

MERGING THE PROPHETIC STREAMS

The prophetic streams can and should be merged. There are those who do not have visions or dreams, and there are those who never hear an audible voice. I believe God wants to merge these different streams of the prophetic. In 1 Samuel 9:9 you can see a picture of this merger:

> Beforetime in Israel, when a man went to enquire of God, thus he spake, Come, and let us go to the seer: for he that is now called a Prophet was beforetime called a Seer.
>
> —KJV

Both Samuel and Nathan were called prophets and seers. When you operate in both streams, it means you flow in both the *nabiy* (speaking forth) and seer (dreams and visions) streams. The seer realm is one of growth. If you look at the above passage, you will see that the title of the office changed from seer to prophet because God was building and expanding the gift. Seers are able to see in the now, and prophets are able to see afar off. They are able to both hear and see. I believe this was the original intent.

Prophets should be able to flow in both streams. Those who hear the audible voice of God should have some type of sight. I am not saying that we have to have great and elaborate visions and go into the second and third heavens, but we should at least have some dreams.

I believe that we all have the ability to have supernatural sight. We need to be able to have elementary or basic dreams and visions. These are usually for our benefit. Dream and visons are useful tools when it comes to warning, correcting, clarity, and direction. In this season, there are many false prophets among us, so it is only going to be to our benefit to ask God to open up our visionary sight so that we can see and operate effectively.

If you haven't done so, this is a good time to ask God to open the eyes of your understanding so you can see Him. As part of your daily prayer, pray according to 2 Kings 6:17—"Lord, open my eyes that I may see"—and Ephesians 1:18—"Lord, open the eyes of my understanding that I may be enlightened; that I may know what is the hope of Your calling, what are the riches of the glory of Your inheritance in the saints."

These prayers and verses will be helpful in getting you activated.

As I developed into the fullness of my prophetic gift, I really wanted to be able to hear as well because I didn't hear like that of a *nabiy* prophet. It actually bothered me for a long time that I couldn't. "Why wasn't I hearing God the way other prophets were hearing Him?" I questioned. So, I prayed and sought God until He gave me both abilities to see and hear.

Remember, every good gift comes from God, and it's important to ask Him for them. I wanted the gifts, so I asked God for them, and He gave them to me. It's beneficial to flow in both streams, but if you don't it does not mean you are any less than those who do. No one is better than another. In the body of Christ, we have a diversity of gifts. Difference does not equate to importance or value.

Chapter Two

CHARACTERISTICS OF THE SEER

As I HAVE just mention, a prophet can be both a seer (*ra'ah*, *chozeh*, and *ro'eh*) and a hearer (*nabiy*) of the messages and revelations from God. Let's first look at the different levels within the seer realm. A great example of these degrees would be found in the books of Daniel and Ezekiel. These men were unique in that they saw great visions. They were taken up into the heavens, and angels interacted with them on different levels. Some seers will not have those types of visions or visitations, yet they are still seers. How one sees and what they see reveals the level of gifting they operate in.

ELABORATE VISIONS

Seers who have very elaborate visions, see deep into the spirit realm, or are taken up into the second or third heavens are very close to God. Let's look at Daniel for instance. He was considered to have a close relationship with God because he prayed all the time. The Bible says that Daniel prayed three times a day even when King Darius signed a decree that said no one could petition any other god or man except King Darius for thirty days. Daniel continued to pray in the manner he was accustomed to. (See Daniel 6:6–10.)

Daniel's was gifted in interpretation of all dreams and all visions. Daniel 5 talks about how King Belshazzar had a great feast and decided that he would use the golden vessels that were taken from Jerusalem by his father Nebuchadnezzar. While drinking from the golden vessels a finger of a man's hand came forth and wrote on the wall of the king's palace. The scripture goes on to say that this troubled the king and he called for all of the soothsayers, astrologers, and interpreters.

> Then came in all the king's wise men: but they could not read the writing, nor make known to the king the interpretation thereof.
> —Daniel 5:8

The queen came to King Belshazzar and told him that there was one who had the spirit and wisdom of the holy gods (v. 11). Daniel was able to read the writing on the wall because he spent time in the presence of God and it was given to him to know the mysteries of heaven.

Wisdom

Wisdom is also a very important characteristic of a seer. There will be some things that God will allow you to see and you may have to bring correction to the people whom the revelation affects. This will require a great deal of supernatural wisdom. You have to learn to bring correction in a way that the people can receive it.

When I started interpreting dreams, I noticed God wanted me to bring correction. A fair amount of dreams I received fell into the category of self-condition or warning dreams. I found myself in a curious position where I was bringing correction on a regular basis.

Correction and wisdom goes hand-in-hand. It is dangerous to give correction without wisdom. It can cause a person to become injured and thus unable to receive the help God is trying to bring to their lives.

The goal of correction is to bring an issue to the forefront so that the person is able to receive the correction and change the behavior. What I am seeing is correction without wisdom resulting in offense, and thereby leaving the person in the same or worse state they started in.

Please pray for wisdom. God promised to give it liberally (James 1:5). The truth is, if you don't have wisdom, you should not be engaging in correction. Here is a quick example of what I mean.

If you are a person who is dealing with fornication, I do not have to say, "You know you are going to hell because you are sleeping with that man/woman. You need to get out his/her bed and house. God is not pleased with you."

Would you receive that from me? No, you would feel condemned and attacked. You would take it easier if I said, "I know that it's difficult for you with that man/woman right now. I know you love them. I know you care about them, and you may feel God sent this person to you, but God doesn't want you in that situation. He loves you too much, and you are precious to Him. He does not want to leave you like this. That situation you are in is not of Him. God wants all of you."

Do you see the difference? There is a way to tell the truth and still be gracious. You have to show a person God's love while bringing the correction God is sending through you. When a rebuke or correction is delivered with wisdom and compassion, the individual can take it in a lot better. You do not want to put a person on the defense and make them turn away from God. The goal is to get them to turn to God.

A lot of prophets have it backward. God is not trying to drive us away with correction. He desires to draw us toward Him with conviction. Correction plants the seed to bring the person home. The Bible tells us, "With lovingkindness have I drawn thee" (Jer. 31:3).

There are times, however, when God will reveal to you a hard word that must be delivered the hard way. When does this happen? Most of the time this happens when a person has refused to hear God and He is giving them a final warning. There are times when I hear God very strong in my ear, saying, "Say it this way." When people are refusing to hear God, He has to come in a stronger more direct way.

God will cover you in your sin, while you are trying to make changes. Unfortunately, there are times when He will say enough is enough and you need to change now. Let me give you an example. There was a lady who lived in my home town and she was severely overweight. The word of the Lord came to her saying that she needed to lose weight. She was aware of this fact but was slow to change. This same lady came to a service and a prophet called her up to the front. He said, "God has tried to warn you in private, but you wouldn't listen. He has been trying to tell you in private, but you won't hear Him. So, God has released me to say this to you: if you don't lose weight, you will surely die. If you don't take the weight off, you will die."

Soon after the prophet delivered this word to her, she went and had weight loss surgery. Not long after having the surgery, she was in a very bad car accident. On that very day, it was the first day the woman was able to put her seat belt on because she had lost enough weight. She was told if she did not have her seat belt on, she would have died.

While it is important to deliver the word of correction in love, it is also true that God will cause a hard word to be delivered strongly and directly. But most of the time a hard word is given when the person has not been listening and will not hear Him.

When prophets are delivering a correcting word, it has to be tempered with wisdom and compassion. Giving a hard and direct word should be the exception and only done under the direction and guidance of the Holy Spirit. When releasing a harsh word, wisdom is still needed. Wisdom is the principle, or first, thing. So, no beating people up in the name of the Lord.

HINDRANCES THE SEER MUST OVERCOME

Having a gift does not exempt you from being injured. As a matter of fact, many gifted people deal with major rejection. Seers who are injured must be healed so that they are not operating out of their own pain. It is very dangerous when a person is set in a ministry position and has not gone through deliverance. Without healing from past hurt, a seer can and will interpret everything they see in a negative or derogatory way. Here are some of the issues seers can internalize that will affect their flow.

A bitter well

I remember watching a seer interpret a dream and everything they said was negative. I spoke with them about this dream and gave them an alternative description. They were truly amazed at how they missed the actual understanding of the dream. We went through a few more dreams, and they could only tell me the interpretation from a negative standpoint. During our discussions, it was discovered that they had been dealing with rejection and had not been healed. They were spiritually unable to discern the positive aspects of the dream because of the influence of the spirit that had them bound and kept them from being able to receive true interpretations.

It is not hard to identify a person who is ministering out of hurt and anger. They speak words that are not edifying to the body of Christ, or they will deliver correction using harsh and demeaning words. These seers need to be healed before they release words so that they will operate effectively.

A spirit of pride

When a prophet or a seer doesn't have the characteristics of love, compassion, or wisdom and they do not spend time in the presence of God, they leave themselves open to the spirit of pride. I believe that pride attacks prophets. And not just prophets, pride also attacks those in leadership. If you are in a position of authority or a spiritual door to major platforms, I believe pride will try to attack you. It is your access to God's people coupled with your elevation that attracts this spirit. This is why you need to stay in a humble position with the Lord.

Many prophets have been captured by this spirit because they began to love the applause of men. Saul was a great example of this. He became jealous when he was not receiving the praises of the people. First Samuel 18:7–8 states:

> The women sang as they played and danced, saying, "Saul has slain his thousands, and David his ten thousands."
>
> Then Saul became very angry, for this saying displeased him; and he said, "They have ascribed to David ten thousands, but to me they have ascribed [only] thousands. Now what more can he have but the kingdom?"
>
> —AMP

People will give you praise thinking that it is because of you they are healed and their lives are being changed. Some won't understand that you are just a vessel God is working through to bring about His purposes. When getting all the applause you have to remember it is not you; it is God.

When I pray, I ask God daily, "Lord, let me decrease so that You may increase." The more you are filled with His Spirit, the less room you have for the flesh. Pride can attack anybody, so you have to stay humble before the Lord. People will applaud you when you are telling them what they want to hear. Then they will stop when you are bringing correction. You should never fall in love with the applause. This will cause you to compromise the position God placed you in. If this word has brought conviction on your heart. Now is a good time to stop, repent, and ask God to place you back in right standing.

When you see a leader operating out of the spirit of pride, you have to pray for them because they are being attacked. This demonic spirit is trying to attach to them to kill their purpose, destiny, and church. Even though they are exhibiting this spirit of pride, it is important to remember we are not fighting against flesh and blood but principalities and powers (Eph. 6:12). We have to pray against the spirit that is trying to kill them. We don't want them, their families, or ministries to die. We have to do more as the body of Christ to cover our leaders in fervent prayer. That is why we also need wise counsel around us. The Bible says there is safety in a multitude of counsel. Prophets should really have other prophets around them. The Word of God says that prophets are subject to other prophets (1 Cor. 14:32). They traveled in companies because they were able to keep each other accountable and judge the words that were heard or images that were seen.

You have to continuously stay in the presence of God so that you will not begin to operate out of the spirit of pride. Prophets are to draw people to God and not to themselves.

Loneliness

Another spirit that attacks prophets is loneliness. I encountered this spirit on several occasions, and the Lord had to teach me how to effectively deal with it. When I was coming up, I had really severe bouts of depression. I would get in my closet at home and sit there and just be depressed and down. I was a different child, and not many people cared to deal with me because of my relationship with God. Needless to say, I did not have a lot of boyfriends and wasn't invited to many parties. My mother would come into the room and ask what's wrong. Because I would be up one day, feeling awesome, and then the next day, depression would hit. My emotions kept swinging like that and it really bothered me.

One day I read a book that talked about prophets' personalities, and it said that prophets are prone to these mood swings. The prophet Elijah would win great victories such as defeating all of Jezebel's false prophets and then he would be running from her. Later, you would find him in the wilderness asking God to kill him because he had enough. (See 1 Kings 19.) Still I was becoming increasingly concerned about these bouts I was having, until the Lord spoke to me and said to pray for balance in my emotions.

This is a critical point for prophets. Some don't believe they should pray for balance, as they feel God made them a certain way. However, the enemy knows how to take specific traits of our personalities and push them into a negative state. Prophets are people with great vision and insight. In particular, it allows them access to personal information about certain people.

Let's look at the Hebrew word *ro'eh* as discussed earlier. Another meaning is "one who is a revealer of secrets, one who envisions."[1] Not many people want to be around a person who can reveal hidden secrets or a person who can see your secret issues as revealed by God. Even though this gift is not constantly in operation, it can be disconcerting for some people.

Lack of mentorship

The lack of mentorship and relatable kindship within the seer realm can be disastrous. The seeing gift is one of major visual encounters with angels, demons, and the like. The seer needs another person who can help define, relate, and confirm their encounters. They have dreams and visions, and God is speaking to them at night. They spend a lot of midnight hours awake in the presence of God, which results in a lack of sleep or rest. It gets lonely when you know you see visions of things far off and ahead of time but are told the visionary encounters, dreams, and visions are not real. It's lonely because you are moving in a realm people are not moving in yet. They don't understand your unique giftings and you are called strange. All of this makes depression a real issue.

As believers, we want to know how we fit into God's kingdom. Prophets have a lot of emotional baggage to carry as we fight through the opposition set against our unique gift. That is why it's important to ask God for strength and to ask for it from some other prophets around you.

I had only one seer friend when I was coming up as a prophet. I used to feel like I was crazy and didn't know what was going on, but after I would call them, I would feel so much better. I would tell them about visions I had and ask, "What do you think?" They would confirm that God had spoken the same thing to them. Just being able to have this small bit of connection with another prophet was such a benefit. I would come away from our conversations rejoicing because I knew I was not imaging things: "God showed me a vision, and I'm not crazy!"

A PROPHET'S SACRIFICE

It's a heavy weight to be a prophet. When I hear a person say they want to be a prophet, I always ask, "Why? Is it because it looks popular?" There are two sides to every gift and some people have no understanding of the sacrifices that some of them require.

When I was a child I was mad at God, seriously mad at Him. I couldn't understand why I couldn't be a certain way or hangout with everybody else. I would feel convicted all the time, especially when I would try to do things others were doing. I wanted to party and get out there, but the Lord would not let me. I tried to rebel, but most of the time it was useless. God was always tugging at me heart to do the right things, which can be difficult for a young person trying to fit in.

One time, I went to a party and was trying to have fun, and I heard the Lord say, "Leave the party."

I was upset, so I sat there still trying to enjoy the party, and I heard the Lord say again, "Leave the party."

I was reluctant to leave, so I stayed a little longer.

A third time, I heard Him say, "Leave the party."

Finally, I got up and went to tell my sister we had to leave the party. She said no, and that she was going to stay. I tried to convince her to leave, but she didn't want to. So I got up, walked out the door, and went down the street by myself. The next thing I knew the police showed up at the house I just left, because the group who were partying was a mixture of college kids and underage minors. We shouldn't have been there, and it worked out for me that God made me get up and leave.

It was always like that for me, so at a certain age I just stopped trying to fit in. When you are young, you can't see what God is doing. It wasn't until later that I realized God was keeping me from making bad decisions. He had a plan for my life and He didn't want me to miss it.

This is a hard road to walk, and sometimes a lonely one. God will pull people away from you so that He can have time with you. Your lonely time is your opportunity to build your relationship with God, time for you to grow in hearing His voice and receiving revelation Him, and time to find your identity in Him. He will bring people along to help with the process in due season. Your alone time is God's time.

I want to leave you with this: prophets and seers do not operate like the false prophets the Bible speaks about. False prophets speak forth words and visions God did not say, and they lead people astray. Ezekiel 13:2–3 says,

> Son of man, prophesy against the prophets of Israel who are now prophesying. Say to those who prophesy out of their own imagination: "Hear the word of the LORD! This is what the Sovereign LORD says: Woe to the foolish prophets who follow their own spirit and have seen nothing!"
>
> —NIV

I know there is a lot of pressure when you are a prophet and people are expecting you to perform for them on demand. You must be careful. You cannot make up dreams and visions or speak forth erroneous words. That is the same as lying on the Holy Spirit. You do not want to do that. Neither pressure nor attention should force you to compromise your integrity or the integrity of God's word. Just be willing to say, "I don't know," or "I don't have a word for you." This is not to condemn but a call to prayer. Prophets should only speak when God is speaking. Do not be pressured to bring forth a word God has not spoken. You are not the people's prophet; you are God's anointed.

Chapter Three

DEMYSTIFYING DREAMS AND VISIONS

THERE ARE MANY who believe that dreams have no real meaning, that they are nothing more than mere figments or fractures of images from conscious daily dealings. However, if we dig into the Bible, we will conclude the opposite. The visionary realm is a place where God speaks and communicates His will while we can perceive it.

> In a dream, in a vision of the night, when deep sleep falleth upon men, in slumbering upon the bed; then he openeth the ears of men, and sealeth their instruction.
> —JOB 33:15–16, KJV

Dreams are a real part of the prophetic realm. They are often neglected because their significance is not taught or talked about in our churches. Although, we hear sermons about Joseph and Daniel, dreams are never the focus. Often it is their struggle, hardships, and rise to greatness that stands out most in our minds. We completely missing the beauty of the dream and vision realm, which was the key to how they accessed their future.

We have neglected this stream of the prophetic, and we have missed out on a realm that God has used throughout the Bible to speak to His people. The Bible holds over 233 scriptures regarding dreams and visions, which is why I am often puzzled when I hear people exclaim that dreams have no meanings or that visions are a thing of the past.

I am sure of this one thing: the Bible is clear that not only are dreams for today, but they will increase—more people will have more dreams.

As I discussed in chapter one there are other streams of the prophetic we must not overlook. For example, in Scripture, you will see different meanings associated with the seer or prophet. Let's revisit these terms:

- *Ra'ah*—"to see," particularly in seeing visions. It also means "to gaze," "look upon," or perceive.

- *Chozeh*—"beholder of the vision," "gazer," or "stargazer"

These terms represent a form of sight or vision. The questions one must ask now are, "Why did God use this stream of the prophetic?" "How can it be used to our advantage?" "Why are we uneducated about it?" and "How do we erase the stigma that comes along with the visionary?"

I often find that this realm is mystified, that we turn it into witchcraft or mysticism. We have a hard time as the body of Christ with things that we cannot understand or have no real experience with. We must begin to move beyond the fear of the unknow and allow God to reveal through His Word the true nature of the visionary. Joel 2:28–29 reads:

> And it shall come to pass afterward, that I will pour out my spirit upon all flesh; and your sons and your daughters shall prophesy, your old men shall dream dreams, your young men shall see visions: And also upon the servants and upon the handmaids in those days will I pour out my spirit.
>
> —KJV

If the Bible is the infallible Word of God, then when He says He will pour out His Spirit in a way that will result in the release of more dreams and visions, it is important to believe God's Word. With the increase of dreams and visions will come a need for interpreters. We have to understand what God is saying. What is it about this realm that it would warrant a release of an extra measure of His Spirit. Could it be that we have a hard time perceiving God? Look at Job 33:14: "Indeed God speaks once, or twice, yet no one notices it."

With the busy lives most people lead, it's no wonder we have a hard time hearing, understanding, or even spending time with God. People have allowed themselves to be consumed, distracted, and focused on everything other than God. We are a technological generation that has replaced time in prayer with idle hours in front of the television or social media. The Lord chooses to wait until we can listen without distraction and speaks to us in a vision of the night. The Scriptures are full of the purpose of dreams and visions and we will explore this further.

PURPOSES FOR DREAMS AND VISIONS

1. To keep us from harm or evil

> From there Abraham journeyed toward the territory of the Negeb and lived between Kadesh and Shur; and he sojourned in Gerar. And Abraham said of Sarah his wife, "She is my sister." And Abimelech king of Gerar sent and took Sarah. But God came to Abimelech in a dream by night and said to him, "Behold, you are a dead man because of the woman whom you have taken, for she is a man's wife."
> —GENESIS 20:1–3

We can ascertain from the passage above the true mercy of God and His willingness to warn us in a dream. He was keeping the king from harm, even death. Sarah was Abraham's wife. Had he not heeded the warning in the dream, he would have surely met his end. It is God's sovereign grace and mercy that would warn even the unbeliever. This is what makes dreams and visions so unique. They are an avenue to reach everyone. Faith is not required. God just needs a person who can dream.

2. To reveal God's will

> Jacob left Beersheba and went toward Haran. And he came to a certain place and stayed there that night, because the sun had set. Taking one of the stones of the place, he put it under his head and lay down in that place to sleep. And he dreamed, and behold, there was a ladder set up on the earth, and the top of it reached to heaven. And behold, the angels of God were ascending and descending on it! And behold, the LORD stood above it and said, "I am the LORD, the God of Abraham your father and the God of Isaac."
> —GENESIS 28:10–13

Just as Jacob received insight from God that God would give him the very ground he laid on and His plan for Jacob's life, God wants to reveal His will to you. Many people have told me on a regular basis that they have no idea what God has planned for their lives. Truthfully many have had dreams and dismissed them as fantasy. Take a fresh look at some of those older dreams. You may be surprised that God was speaking His will into your life all along.

3. To encourage us

> "Behold, I dreamed a dream, and behold, a cake of barley bread tumbled into the camp of Midian and came to the tent and struck it so that it fell and turned it upside down, so that the tent lay flat." And his comrade answered, "This is no other than the sword of Gideon the son of Joash, a man

of Israel; God has given into his hand Midian and all the camp."

As soon as Gideon heard the telling of the dream and its interpretation, he worshiped. And he returned to the camp of Israel and said, "Arise, for the LORD has given the host of Midian into your hand."

—JUDGES 7:13–15

In Judges chapter 7, we find the story of Gideon, a very timid man, who was able to do extraordinary things for God all because he heard a dream. Gideon overheard a dream that was given to the enemy's camp. The dream said that Gideon would win the fight. This greatly encouraged him. It gave him so much strength in fact that they were able to defeat the Midianites with just one hundred men. You will be encouraged to follow through with God's instructions even if you are fearful. God can send you what you need to hear to strengthen you for the battle ahead.

4. To reveal the future

Have you ever thought, "If God would have just told me that the flood, droughts, or natural disasters were coming, I would have done some things differently"? Have you every thought, "If He would have warned me ahead of time, I could have prepared"? Dreams can reveal the future. In Genesis 41 Pharaoh had one such dream.

> After two whole years, Pharaoh dreamed that he was standing by the Nile, and behold, there came up out of the Nile seven cows, attractive and plump, and they fed in the reed grass. And behold, seven other cows, ugly and thin, came up out of the Nile after them, and stood by the other cows on the bank of the Nile. And the ugly, thin cows ate up the seven attractive, plump cows. And Pharaoh awoke.
>
> —V. 1–4

This dream was interpreted by one of the most famous interpreters in the Bible—Joseph. This dream revealed that a drought was coming upon the land. Had Pharaoh ignored this dream, it would have been detrimental to the Egyptian people. However, God had greater plans. He wanted to save Egypt so that He could in fact save His own people.

When God reveals the future, it is for His agenda. One of the greatest avenues He uses is dreams. We can see this same pattern for King Nebuchadnezzar in Daniel 2. The king had a dream that greatly disturbed him. He called for all his wise men to reveal this dream. The passage tells us there was only one man—Daniel—who was able to interpret the dream. His also foretold of future kingdoms and their eventual demise.

Once again God revealed the future through dreams to move forward His own plan—a plan that revealed Daniel's God.

5. To instruct

If we look in the Book of Matthew chapter 1, it states:

> And her husband Joseph, being a just man and unwilling to put her to shame, resolved to divorce her quietly. But as he considered these things, behold, an angel of the Lord appeared to him in a dream, saying, "Joseph, son of David, do not fear to take Mary as your wife, for that which is conceived in her is from the Holy Spirit."
>
> —vv. 19–20

The angel of the Lord came and delivered to Joseph instructions concerning Mary and what he needed to do in regard to her. He was ready to divorce her. But in a dream, he was given specific instruction on what to do and how to handle his current situation.

In Acts 9 when Saul was stopped on the road to Damascus, you mostly hear about his conversion from one who persecuted the Jews to one of the greatest apostles of all time. But we neglect the audible voice of God that he and his men heard that gave them clear instruction on how to move forward.

In that same scenarios we encounter Annais, who was shown a vision of Paul and given instruction on where to find him, what he looked like, and what he should do once he encountered him.

In these examples, we see that one of the purposes of dreams and visions is to instruct the dreamer or visionary. God will show up for us in times when we need to make important decisions. How many times did God use a dream to instruct you to leave a person alone or to change jobs, but we dismissed it because we felt it was just a dream.

6. To bring warning

There are several instances in Scripture where warnings have been given through these distinct avenues. When we look at the prophet Ezekiel, he was given many visons from God to warn the children Israel of their rebellion. Ezekiel opens with a great vision from heaven that shows the majesty and miraculous nature of the One who sits on the throne. Then He spoke to Ezekiel saying,

> Son of man, I send thee to the children of Israel, to a rebellious nation that hath rebelled against me: they and their fathers have transgressed against me, even unto this very day.
> For they are impudent children and stiffhearted. I do send thee unto them; and thou shalt say unto them, Thus saith the Lord God.
> —EZEKIEL 2:3–4, KJV

Throughout this entire book, Ezekiel was sent many visions of warning and judgment for Israel. God will speak to us to place us back on the right track, to stop us from sinning against Him, and to return us back to Himself. Warning dreams are often considered bad things. But when you truly look at them, warning dreams are loving correction sent from the Father to guide us and give us opportunity to correct the situation that will cause our eventual destruction.

7. To bring adjustment to our thinking

Perhaps we have adopted a view point that is contrary to God's vision or thinking. This requires a paradigm shift. The Lord will bring a dream or vision to adjust your way of seeing a particular thing or even the way you view the world. Peter was a great man of God. He was an advocate for the faith and a true disciple of our Lord Jesus. However, he adopted a worldview that the Lord did not want him to have. It was outdated. With the emergence of our Lord, there were laws that had been fulfilled and a new testament that would soon emerge.

One thing we have discovered is that before anything can truly change, the first shift must be in our mind-set. Peter was a Jew, and as such he was raised with certain beliefs and ideologies of who was clean or unclean. So, the Lord sent a vision of a sheet descending with animals that were unclean. He told Peter to rise, kill, and eat (Acts 11:7).

For Jews during this time, the animals he saw were considered unclean and he was forbidden to partake of them. Eating them would defile him, but God was shifting his paradigm. He was explaining that there was a new foundation being laid, and God was expressing this great truth through a dream.

Dreams are the foundation of many scriptures in the Bible, over 233 are dedicated to the function of this realm. With that being said, in order to benefit from the seer realm, one must dream, which leads us into our next question.

WHO HAS THE ABILITY TO DREAM, AND DOES THAT ALONE MAKE A PROPHET?

This is a question that must be dealt with on some level so that we have a clear understanding of the function and operation. Let's first deal with the first part of this initial question: who has the ability to dream?

Some schools of thought teach that only Christians can hear from God, therefore you can only receive prophetic dreams if you have received salvation. Clearly, this cannot be the proper conclusion if we look to the Scriptures as an authority.

Genesis 41, tells the account of Joseph, a dreamer and interpreter of dreams. His life led him on a long path that eventually culminate with an encounter with the pharaoh of Egypt. Pharaoh had a troubling dream that he could not understand. This brought much attention to Joseph who was able to come and give revelation as to what the dream represented. This is a great example of an unbeliever who was able to receive a prophetic vision from the God of heaven.

If we look a little further, our studies will take us to an account in Genesis 20:3:

> But God came to Abimelech in a dream by night and said to him, "Behold, you are a dead man because of the woman whom you have taken, for she is a man's wife."
>
> —KJV

Abimelech was given a dream, and not even one that needed interpretation by an interpreter but was interpreted by God Himself. He revealed to Abimelech the grave danger he was in if he was to move forward with his plans to take Sarah as his wife. In this instance God crossed a barrier we placed upon Him and delivered a life-saving message right to the heart of this unbelieving man. Many of us may forget this, but you cannot box God in.

These examples also answer the second part of the question: does the ability to dream make one a prophet? The answer is no.

Abimelech was a heathen king. The Bible tells us that he was not of Jewish descent and was one who did not acknowledge the God of Israel. However, God showed him mercy and caused him to have a dream that revealed to him Abraham and Sarah's true relationship. As we see from the verse above, Abimelech had a clear conscious and was, in fact, innocent as it pertained his taking Abraham's wife. Abraham chose to disclose only the partial truth about his wife Sarah out of his own fear of death. The other reason God gave Abimelech this dream was because it helped to further the plans and purposes God had for Abraham and Sarah. It was also a display of His mercy.

As mentioned earlier in this book, there are specific criteria to one being called to the office of a prophet. You can refer to that section in the introduction under "Are You a Dreamer?" for more detailed information. I want to stress again that the ability to have a dream from God is not predicated on a prophetic office, but dreams are tools that have been given to believers and unbelievers alike.

I love the fact there are no restrictions when it comes to this realm. God allows Himself to be seen by believers and unbelievers alike. This is exciting news. First, we can see that we all have the ability to interact with God on a supernatural level. Maybe you have a hard time hearing God with your spiritual ears. Now you know that you may be one who can see prophecy in motion with your eyes.

Second, this means that we can also use the gift of interpretation as a tool to evangelize the world. Could you imagine how many people would come to Christ just because you explained their dream? I listen to a broadcast when John Paul Jackson was the guest. He talked about the work his team did with psychics and those who practiced this type of witchcraft. He gave great detail of his involvement with evangelizing this group. They would set up tents and allow people to experience God in various ways.

When I heard how they went out in the world to effect change through dreams and visions, it totally transformed the way I see the church. It's time that we seek God for unconventional ways to reach unconventional people. I, as a strong believer, know that this can be accomplished through dreams and visions.

Chapter Four

HOW THE SEER GIFT POSITIONS YOU

DREAMS AND VISIONS are an integral part of the prophetic realm. We have heard countless numbers of sermons about Joseph the dreamer, where we are led to understand his pit-to-palace experience, but what about his ability to accurately interpret dreams? It was specifically this gift of interpretation that positioned him. It was this gift that saved Egypt and ultimately secured him a position next to Pharaoh.

Genesis 41 tells the story of Joseph's encounter with pharaoh when he was called before him to interpret a dream no one else was able to understand. In this example, a strong signal is sent about the uniqueness of this gift. Joseph's ability to understand dreams was not something even the soothsayers could imitate. You have to truly have a connection or relationship with the Creator of all the earth to reveal or decode His messages from heaven. Job 33:23 states: "If there be a messenger with him, an interpreter, one among a thousand, to shew unto man his uprightness" (KJV).

The rareness of this gift—"one among a thousand"—can give us some clue as to the importance of this gift. It is not a gift that is given to everyone, but it is a gift that should be coveted as a tool that will lead and direct men with instruction and insight direct from the heart of God.

Joseph's obedience to God and his willingness to interpret dreams no matter what state he found himself in prepared him to stand before pharaoh confident in his ability to interpret. What is even more astonishing is that pharaoh himself had to recognize that Joseph's God was the true, living God who would not only give a dream but also send an interpreter to decode it. Then Joseph's gift and ability to hear from heaven caused him to be placed in a high position of power in a foreign land. We see here that dreams and visions can put people in positions of influence.

With Daniel, however, it was not the interpretation gift alone but a combination of factors that led to his longevity. In Daniel chapter 1, we are given a closer look at other key factors that played an important role to his advancement in a foreign kingdom.

UNDEFILED SEERS ARE PROMOTED

> But Daniel purposed in his heart that he would not defile himself with the portion of the king's meat, nor with the wine which he drank: therefore, he requested of the prince of the eunuchs that he might not defile himself.
>
> —KJV

One of the key characteristics when it comes to being placed in a prominent position is to determine within yourself that you will not defile yourself with worldly pleasures. Daniel was offered a portion from the king's own table. Normally this would be a great honor, but to Daniel it would mean the breaking of God's laws. When faced with challenges in a foreign land, Daniel did not place his God over on a shelf and walk away. Many times, we find ourselves compromising our standards to get along. However, Daniel knew there was danger in compromise and that could only lead to more destruction. So, he put his faith in God and took his chances with angering the overseer. We must always remember, as God places us into positions in the marketplace, there will be many different gods, but we cannot compromise our Christianity to get along.

Take the parable of the ox for example in 2 Corinthians 6:14:

> Do not be unequally yoked with unbelievers. For what partnership has righteousness with lawlessness? Or what fellowship has light with darkness?

This scripture reminds us to not be unequally yoked with unbelievers. But when we look further in the scripture, we must understand this parable. Oxen had to be equally yoked, meaning you could not have a weaker animal and a stronger animal tied together. (See Deuteronomy 22:10.) When you have a donkey and ox tied together, you have a recipe for disaster. The donkey being shorter and lighter and the ox being taller and stronger would put undue stress on the ox. When you have this combination the weaker of the animals is going to cause the stronger animal to work harder. Therefore, it is important to allow for the equal distribution of work by yoking animals with the same strength and stamina.

Why is this important in the case of Daniel? When God wants to position us for greatness, He must trust that we will be strong in our faith. He does not want us to be unequally yoked. He wants us to walk in our full potential and to do this we must be able to push back the food of the world, so to speak.

In verse 12 Daniel made a bold request. He said, "Prove thy servants, I beseech thee, ten days; and let them give us pulse to eat, and water to drink." This bold declaration indicate that he was sure God would not fail him.

We must be able to stand in the face of pressure to conform. We cannot allow the enemy to overpower us. We must be firm in our convictions, so that God can trust us to stand in the face of evil and not waiver. How can He release us to higher or greater positions if we are not rooted and grounded in Him?

Matthew 25:23 says, "His master said to him, 'Well done, good and faithful servant. You have been faithful over a little; I will set you over much. Enter into the joy of your master.'" It was this faithfulness that released the gifts these Hebrew young men needed for where they were going. By their bold actions, they proved that they would stand faithful to God even while in captivity in a strange land. Because of this, God continued to show them favor by giving them "learning and skill in all literature and wisdom, and Daniel had understanding in all visions and dreams" (v. 17, KJV).

Where the four were going, God knew what gifts they would needed to excel. Wisdom and learning He gave to all, but to only one, He gave the understanding of all dreams and all visions. This simple edge that God released to Daniel caused him to advance to one of the highest positions in a foreign kingdom. He was an asset because of his gift. As we become more fluent in our seer gifts, many of us will be welcomed into the inner circle of decision makers in high places. There, we will provide the wise counsel that will lead others to prosper and come to know the power of God.

SEERS REVEAL DESTINY AND GIVE HOPE FOR THE FUTURE

Many people are wondering who God has called them to be, where they are going, and who they are. This is why they need to grab hold of dreams and visions. The dreams and visions we have as seer have are designed to replace negative words that were spoken over the person's life. A prime example is a person who has grown up in a dysfunctional or abusive home. They may have heard certain words all their life, words such as, "You are stupid," "You are not loved," "No one cares about you." God will use a dream or vision to replace the curse that was heard by the ear with a visual prophecy or true vision of who God created you to be!

I call this process replacement therapy. This process involves opening up your spiritual eyes, through reciting certain scriptures, praying, and fasting. This process seeks out God for a dream—which we can call a calling or destiny dream—related to your purpose or your gift. Normally, this process can also be accompanied by deliverance when necessary. Since visions are so powerful having this type of overriding experience will displace the negative words and give the dreamer renewed hope for their future.

Moses saw a vision that restored his hope for a once-defeated people.

In Exodus 3, Moses had lost hope for his people. He was content to be among the Midian people. He had seen the plight of his people and felt the sting of their captivity. But then Moses had a vision of a burning bush, in which God spoke to him and gave him instructions on how to release Israel from captivity. It was this vision that replaced the hopelessness Moses felt about their situation. This vision was so strong that it helped Moses overcome his own insecurities. He was born with a speech impediment, but the power of the vision overruled the embarrassment he felt and gave him the courage to rise above his own limitations. The vision Moses had ultimately sustained him throughout his journey to defeat pharaoh and bring victory to a once defeated people. This same principle can be applied to Jacob the trickster.

Jacob saw a vision that gave him a new identity and changed the trajectory of his life.

In Genesis 27, with Esau's birthright in hand, Jacob and his mother devised a scheme. Disguised as Esau (wearing his brother's clothing and attaching animal skins to his arms and neck), Jacob provided a counterfeit meal for his blind father to replace the one Esau was supposed to prepare. He then announced to his blind father, "I am Esau your firstborn. I have done as you told me; now sit up and eat of my game, so that you may bless me" (v. 19).

This is not the first time we see Jacob plot against his brother and trick him out of his birthright. And after this instance, he fled and was on the run, in fear for his life. Then he had a vision from God of a ladder that ascended and descended, and the Lord stood beside him and pronounced a blessing over him (Gen. 28:12–17).

This vision from God changed Jacob's entire life. He went from a man who had no future and no hope, a man who was a liar and a thief, to a man chosen by God to walk in mega favor. However, the real importance of dreams and visions are contained in their power to sustain.

Joseph saw dreams and visions that sustained him through the most difficult moments in life.

Dreams and vision will sustain us through the tough times of life. Joseph is well known to most Christians. We know of his many famous dreams, but what we haven't explored is how the dreams he had as a young child, sustained him through his adult life. We are tempted to believe that because Joseph was shown favor in Potiphar's house and even in the prison, that this is what allowed him to keep his sanity through the times when he was forcibly sold in to slavery, slandered by Potiphar's wife, worked tirelessly in a prison, and lost the dignity that once graced his life.

However, I believe it was the dreams that God had given him at a young age that sustained him as God's promise manifested. He was not only a dreamer but also an interpreter of dreams. He knew to some extent what his dreams meant. These dreams had to come to past, for they were given by the true God. When Joseph revealed to his brothers who he really was, he said something very shocking:

> Do not be afraid, for am I in God's place? As for you, you meant evil against me, but God meant it for good in order to bring about this present result, to preserve many people alive.
>
> —Genesis 50:19–20, NIV

Joseph received a revelation. He finally understood that all the trials and tribulations were to bring to fruition his vision as a child.

SEERS SEE VISIONS THAT SUSTAIN

Could you imagine finally coming into face-to-face contact with your betrayers and having enough restraint to forgive them for the harm they intentionally tried to cause you? This would be impossible if you did not have a vision to sustain you. Because so many of us need to get a vision like this, I want us to walk through the life of Joseph to get a better understanding of a vision that sustains us through life's most challenging times.

In the Book of Genesis, we are given a chronicle of the events that took place in Joseph's life. The first conflicts we see happen between Joseph and his brother are a result of his father's favoritism and his unique gift of dreaming dreams and seeing visions. His brothers despised him and sought out ways to destroy him.

The vision we are most acquainted with is found in Genesis 37:7: "For behold, we were binding sheaves in the field, and lo, my sheaf rose up and also stood erect; and behold, your sheaves gathered around and bowed down to my sheaf" (KJV). This vision caused the most controversy among the family, but it was the dream that would be the saving grace of the nation.

It's ironic how the dream that causes people to hate you is the very dream that will catapult you into your destiny.

Joseph knew that his dreams and visions were messages that were calling out the greatness in him. He was aware that he was different than his brothers. He knew he was called out by the very God of the universe. Still, at some point, the brother's jealousy and envy took hold of them and caused a conspiracy to be birthed. Joseph's brothers plotted to murder him and throw him in a pit. They carried out part of their plan, and left Joseph in a very grave situation. I believe that the vision God had spoken over his life was the only thing that kept him from losing his mind and giving into the fear of death.

This vision gave him strength as he was sold off into slavery to a faraway land—a place he had never been. When he was sold to the highest bidder, he may have thanked God he was put into a good house with a wealthy man. But can you imagine the despair and rejection he must have suffered from? Betrayal and abuse from one's own family is some of the hardest to bear. Thankfully, He soon found favor in Potiphar's house.

Maybe Joseph thought, "OK, well, maybe this is it. The dream I had as a young child is coming to pass. I am in charge of Potiphar's house. He is a man of influence and great importance. This must be my time." However, betrayal would soon darken his door of his life once again.

As Joseph was wrongly accused and thrown into prison, His thoughts had to go back to the vision he had as a boy—the vision that showed him he would one day be a person of great importance.

In prison, Joseph soon found favor with the guards, he interpreted dreams, and because of his gift, he came across an opportunity that could possibly get him out of prison. One of the men he spoke to was a man of great importance who could get him out of the prison.

Some time passed, and I believe that Joseph recalled that dream on several occasions, remembering the details and recalling the images right down to the smells. Visions are so powerful. You can recall them and live them over and over again. This is what Joseph did as he held on to the promise of his vision that the Lord spoke over his life at a young age.

Finally released from prison, he stood before Pharaoh. I believe that he stood there thinking, "This is what I have been waiting for my whole life." He must have thought he was seeing his dreams and visions coming to pass right in front of his eyes, but as it turns out he was only seeing it partially revealed. It would not be until his brothers' appearance that he would see the full promise of his vision play out.

Dreams and visions such as the ones Joseph and the others in his story had have long moved nations forward, advanced kingdoms, saved many from harm, and placed people in positions of power and authority. We are in an age where the voice of God is being muted in our nations. We have a clear opportunity to open up a realm of the spirit and allow God to continue to flow through us.

MORE THAN NIGHTTIME FOLLY

Too often people will dismiss their dreams or visions as nothing more than nighttime folly, but they are a valuable and direct line to the heart and mind of God concerning us. Sometime ago, I had a dream about a prophet friend of mine. At the time they were trying to decide if they would join a particular church. In my dream, I saw that if they joined this particular assembly, it would lead them down a particular path that would be detrimental to their spiritual life. Specifically, a spirit of confusion that was being held at bay would be loosed in their life. I had this dream on two occasions, and each time I was diligent in revealing it and its meaning to my friend.

Unfortunately, they did not head the prophetic word birthed through the dreams. I literally watched as this demonic spirit of rebellion has taken their life and now they have adopted a view of God that is contrary to Scripture.

Dreams and visions are often dismissed as simple images birthed through bad eating or nighttime folly. When they are actually prophecy spoken through a movie lens. More than 80 percent of what we perceive in our everyday lives is communicated through our sight or vision. Hearing has a retention rate of about 30 percent. This means that we are more likely to retain or remember what we see.

In 2 Corinthians 10:5 we read about imaginations: "Casting down imaginations, and every high thing that exalteth itself against the knowledge of God, and bringing into captivity every thought to the obedience of Christ" (KJV). This scripture illustrates how hard it is to displace a vision once it's embedded in our minds. These images get so embedded that we have to, in fact, pull them or cast them down. According to *A Bible Commentary for English Readers*, it is a forceful pulling down of a stronghold.[1] When God gives you a vision or dream for your life, it becomes so embedded in your consciousness that even if you wanted to, you could not easily displace it.

Dreams and visions are being used to speak to people all around the world about the things God has in mind for them—from salvation and a revelation of Christ to life callings and vocations. There are visions being reported by Muslims and Jews alike that are leading them to proclaim Jesus as Lord. I have seen products being downloaded in dreams and companies following through to gain significant wealth. There is an urgent need in the earth for the body of Christ to tap into the dream realm and bring down God's plans and strategies. By returning the value to the dreams and visions we have, we will no longer miss out on much needed information for the future.

Chapter Five

HOW WE LOST THE ABILITY TO SEE

THERE IS A doctrine that is being taught that God no longer used dreams and visions as a means to communicate with people. As a matter of fact, many are saying that dreams have no meaning at all. This view is widely held by those who feel that, with the emergence of the Holy Spirit, we have no further need for dreams and visions. They even see interpretation and interpreters as things of a forgotten past. With this thinking in place, there has been little teaching in the area of dreams and vision. When there is no teaching, it is impossible for knowledge to be spread. As Hosea 4:6 says, "My people are destroyed for lack of knowledge: because thou hast rejected knowledge, I will also reject thee, that thou shalt be no priest to me" (KJV).

Having knowledge of a particular avenue that God uses to speak forth His prophecies should be important to His children. If the enemy is allowed to pervade certain areas, not only will we leave this wellspring untapped, but also we leave it to become prey to the enemy's devices.

You can search the internet today and see the prevalence of the enemy's influence in the realm of dreams and visions. Certain websites will speak of spirituality, but they are totally "me centered," and they definitely do not point you in the direction of God.

The seer realm has long since been used by psychics, witches, mediums, and spirits. They have illegally accessed this realm and used it to consult with demonic spirits. We can see this scenario play out in the life of King Saul.

King Saul and the Witch of Endor

Saul was the king of Israel, however, he was replaced by David because he made many decisions that were contrary to what God wanted for His people. Saul would not heed the voice of God. Therefore God would no longer speak with him.

In 1 Samuel 28, we see where Saul was about to face the Philistine army. He was panicked and needed to hear from God before engaging the enemy. At this time, the prophet Samuel, his most trusted advisor, was deceased. How would he hear from God?

> And when Saul saw the host of the Philistines, he was afraid, and his heart greatly trembled and when Saul enquired of the Lord, the Lord answered him not, neither by dreams, nor by Urim, nor by prophets.
>
> —vv. 5–6, kjv

Saul had been completely cut off from the voice of God, but he had become accustomed to having some type of prophetic guidance in carrying out the tasks of the kingdom. Saul was desperate for a word from the spirit realm. Without any of the approved ways to reach God available to him, what would Saul do? He decided to take matters into his own hands. He inquired of a witch.

> Then said Saul unto his servants, Seek me a woman that hath a familiar spirit, that I may go to her, and enquire of her. And his servants said to him, Behold, there is a woman that hath a familiar spirit at Endor.
>
> —v. 7, kjv

Saul was so desperate to hear from God that he consulted a woman with a familiar spirit. This is expressly forbidden by God as evidenced by Leviticus 19:31: "Do not turn to mediums or necromancers; do not seek them out, and so make yourselves unclean by them: I am the LORD your God."

What would make a king desperate enough to break God's commandments? Could this be why even God-fearing Christians would turn to psychic lines or tarot card readers, because some of us have not been empowered to hear what the Lord is saying through dreams and visions?

This breach coupled with other transgressions from God's teachings cost Saul his life and the very life of his sons. He had Samuel called up from his resting place beyond the grave and spoke with him concerning his inability to hear from God.

> And Samuel said to Saul, Why hast thou disquieted me, to bring me up? And Saul answered, I am sore distressed; for the Philistines make war against me, and God is departed from me, and answereth me no more, neither by prophets, nor by dreams: therefore I have called thee, that thou mayest make known unto me what I shall do.
> —1 SAMUEL 28:16, KJV

He said to Samuel, "God no longer answers me through dreams or the prophets" (v. 17, author's paraphrase). This was a great concern to Saul that heaven was shut up from him so that he could not hear.

WITHOUT DREAMS AND VISION, PEOPLE BECOME DESPERATE

When the gift of dreams dies or is cut off and no one is operating in it, people will become desperate. When there are dreams but no interpreters, prophecy dies, and therefore, a gaping hole is left in the prophetic realm. When dreams eluded Saul he turned to those with familiar spirits. Could we say the same thing happened in the church? With the lack of understanding concerning the seer realm, the gift ceased its operation and made room for the occult to take over.

If people are not taught that this is a realm we can use to hear God, then people will do what Saul did. They will consult the psychics. They will flock to those with familiar spirits.

We see this playing out in our society today. Psychics and witchcraft are invading every corner of our societies because we have left this realm to those who have no light in them. We lost the gift because we have stopped believing that it is an approved avenue through which God speaks. Dreams have long been cherished gifts to the believer, but now because of the strong demonic influence, we find that many are afraid and are operating in sinister supernatural folly instead of God-breathed prophecy.

It is important to begin teaching about the seer realm again. We have to stir up the gift as mentioned in 2 Timothy. This gift does not belong to the kingdom of darkness, but it has and forever will be a part of God's kingdom.

How to Regain Access to the Visionary Realm

Wisdom is an important part of the interpretation gift, and to the gift of dreams overall. It takes spiritual wisdom to understand dark sayings or parabolic language. Dreams language is considered a form of parabolic speech, which means that it often needs interpretation. Job 33:14–16 says,

> Indeed God speaks once, or twice, yet no one notices it. In a dream, a vision night, when sleep falls on men, while they slumber in their beds, then He opens the ears of men, and seals their instruction.
>
> —NASB

The word *parable* is found over fifty-five times in Scripture. It was often used to bring understanding of godly principles to the children of God, often hiding its meaning from outsiders or nonbelievers.

With the release of the Holy Spirit in this dispensation, we now have access to greater understanding of His mysteries. With so many people having dreams and visions, we need men and woman who are capable of understanding the messages that God is releasing upon the face of the earth.

Interpretation of parables and dark sayings is not just handed out to anyone. It requires a close walk with God in order for Him to trust us with revelation. Here are some steps you can take if you want to regain access to the dream and vision realm if you've notice any hindrance to your flow. You can also follow these steps if you know you have the gift but have never flowed in it they you know God intends.

1. Ask for wisdom.

As I mentioned above, wisdom is key to understanding and interpreting dreams and visions. We sometimes overlook the spiritual significance of the dreams we have, but wisdom will help us to discern the hidden things of God. Daniel 2:22 says, "He reveals deep and hidden things; he knows what is in the darkness, and the light dwells with him." And in James 1:5, we learn that we can ask God for wisdom and He will give it to us without limit.

2. Press into the glory.

So any one of us may say, "God, I want to have more visions."

He says, "You have to pray more, fast more, and sacrifice more."

God wants us to give ourselves over to Him completely. Some of us may get deeper visions because of the level of our surrender, the ministry office we hold (Eph. 4:11), or what God has purposed for our destinies. However, we encounter some supernatural experiences because our Father in heaven is rewarding us. God says, "I am a rewarder of those who diligently seek Me" (Heb. 11:6). Thus, it is possible to get a gift because you are pressing into the glory.

Look at Daniel or Samuel who dedicated their lives to God. They lived their lives uprightly. When you live a dedicated, holy, upright life before God, He will give you the desires of your heart.

Consider Joseph. He walked in abundant favor with God, and this positioned his life for greatness. We will discuss this more in later chapters.

We have to learn how God and His kingdom operates. I have heard people say that we don't have to do anything to receive from God, but you do have to do some things.

3. Obey.

Moses didn't go into the Promise Land because he was disobedient to what God told him to do. Obedience is one of things that will move you further. Because of His obedience, Joshua replaced Moses and led God's people. His obedience shifted him from obscurity to notoriety. Obedience is a key ingredient in building a close relationship with God.

4. Pray.

But, did you know that a healthy prayer life is key to a relationship with God. The Bible says that Daniel prayed three times a day no matter what (Dan. 6). His prayer life was indispensable to him. His relationship with God was such that he not only interpreted dreams, but he was also given special insight to know what was dreamed without being told. This was a special gift God gave Daniel as a reward for seeking Him out.

The time you spend in God's presence—being more selfless and decidedly saying, "God, my life is Yours,"—will release new realms of the Spirit upon you.

5. Love God's people.

Let me say this: there are too many prophets who do not have compassion or love for God's people. Many times in Scripture when Jesus did great miracles, it says, "...and Jesus was moved with compassion." When people were hungry and in need, compassion for their needy state came first. Then a miracle took place.

You cannot dislike God's people and think He is going to sit you in a high position over them. You cannot be so proud and haughty to think that God is going to put you over His people to injure them, beat them up, and or make them feel bad about their sin. We all have sinned and come short of the glory of God (Rom. 3:23). Convicting the heart of men is different from condemning them to a life sentence. Correction in love is different from prideful condemnation.

You have to have a heart of compassion for God's people *and* you have to be able to tell the truth. If you are not a truthful person you are going to have an issue doing the things that God requires of you. A good question to ask yourself is, "How much love do I have for the people of God? Do I really love them?" Listen, God really loves us, and if you are a person who is always saying, "Destroy them, God," you might need more of God's compassion in your life. If you want everybody struck down, you might need more compassion. If you feel like everybody should be going to hell, you might need a little more compassion. If you are always the person correcting... You get my point. There is a way to say and do anything, but it all has to be done with love.

Look at Moses the Bible says that God spoke to him face to face. That is a gift for the amount of time, perseverance, and suffering he went through. He spent so much time in God's presence that the Bible says he had to veil his face. Moses was a lover of the Lord's people. God wanted to destroy the people, but Moses prayed asking God not to unleash His wrath but to forgive them. He told God that He wouldn't get the glory from their lives if He destroyed them. Moses even went as far as to ask God to forgive their sin, and if not, to blot his name out of the book it was written in. (See Exodus 32:32.)

There are things that God gives you when you have more compassion and love, and more time in His presence and studying His Word. What is your sacrifice to God? Some people are not willing to give up their lives that way. Some tell God either through words or action, "I can give You part of it, but not all of it." If you are person who holds back, you have to understand that your actions in this case are directly affect the operation of your gift. Your gifting cannot exceed the level of your sacrifice.

Chapter Six

A GOOD CHARACTER

ROMANS 11:29 SAYS, "For the gifts and calling of God are without repentance" (KJV), meaning a person can operate in their gift with some character flaws and still effect people lives. But is that good enough for God's people? How can we be satisfied with operating on just the residue of God's glory? How can we be OK with a dullness of sight when operating in the seer realm? We need to be operating in the full measure of God's glory, brilliant, accurate, on point, and full of God's love and righteousness in order to be truly effective against the kingdom of darkness.

It is a dangerous game to try to walk in the gifts of God without purity and integrity, trying to see how close we can get to a line before we cross it. Yet every day we see people more and more willing to live sin-filled lives and play Russian roulette with their spiritual lives. Having a good and upright character has been greatly underplayed and undervalued in this day and age, but God will not endure it for long. Too many lives are at stake.

As we get into this discussion about coupling our gift with strong character, let's first define what character is. Character is the mental and moral qualities distinctive to an individual. These qualities or attributes are key to our ability to shift levels in God and are directly related to degree of gifts that God will release to us.

When I think of character I have to look to the Book of Daniel. When I was coming up in my younger years there were two books of the Bible I spent a lot of time studying. One was the book of 1 Samuel, and the other was of course was Daniel.

I truly believe that the Book of Daniel is a prophet's greatest book. Daniel's character and relationship with God is one that should be studied and followed for those of us who want to walk in true accuracy in the prophetic realm. We often neglect the importance of character and relationship with God when dealing with the release of revelatory gifts. Let's explore revelatory gifts and how the state of our characters connects to the degree of power in which we walk in the seer realm.

GOD REWARDS THE FAITHFUL ONES WITH GIFTS

Revelatory gifts can be found in 1 Corinthians 12:8–10. They are:

- Word of knowledge—supernatural revelation as to a piece of knowledge that would be naturally unknown to the recipient

- Word of wisdom—supernatural impartation of wisdom beyond the natural wisdom of the recipient

- Discerning of spirits—a God-given ability to distinguish the spirit motivating or controlling a person or event

These gifts are key to interpretation of dreams and visions. These are also the gifts Daniel possessed, and I believe they were given to him as a reward for his character and integrity. Let's look at how this happened.

In the Book of Daniel, we are introduced to Daniel and his companions and find them in the Babylonian kingdom after they were taken into captivity. There, they were given new names and were told that they would have to adapt to a new way of life. During this time, Daniel made up his mind that he would walk in the ways of the Lord, no matter what he had to face. He held on to this determination even when he and his companions were told that they would have to eat a certain diet that went against Jewish laws and customs. Daniel 1:8 says,

> But Daniel made up his mind that he would not defile himself with the king's choice food or with the wine which he drank; so, he sought permission from the commander of the officials that he might not defile himself.

We see the great strength of Daniel's character and his resolve to stand by God's word even if it cost him his life. Daniel understood that there could be no compromise when it came it his spiritual life, he served the God of the universe and his commitment to him had to be stronger than his commitment to his flesh. He understood that compromise with ungodly things is what led Israel down the path that led them to the Babylonian captivity in the first place.

Another attribute of Daniel's character was his strong faith. He not only believed he should follow God's plan, but he was also willing to put these principles to the test. He had faith that if God said it, it had to work. Daniel petitioned the overseer to allow them to eat the food that was right for their diet. He even challenged the officials to test them to see if they were not healthier than the other trainees in the kingdom. Daniel 1:12–13 says,

> Please test your servants for ten days and let us be given some vegetables to eat and water to drink. Then let our appearance be observed in your presence and the appearance of the youths who are eating the king's choice food; and deal with your servants according to what you see.
> —NASB

Many times, we say that we believe God, but when it comes time to remain steadfast and faithful in the presence of nonbelievers, we tend to shrink back. Daniel was bold in his faith and was willing to put his God to the test, showing everyone his God was greater.

Daniel demonstrates for us the boldness we should walk in as believers. Essentially, Daniel said, "Watch us and then deal with your servants according to what you see." He trusted that God would show up on their behalf. He was showing his companions as well that they would stand with God and He would come through. He was not going to go down the same path his people took that led to destruction.

After the days had passed, God showed Himself strong on behalf of the four Jewish boys. Because they showed great character, God rewarded them openly. Daniel 1:17 says, "As for these four children, God gave them knowledge and skill in all learning and wisdom: and Daniel had understanding in all visions and dreams" (KJV).

When looking at the text above, we can see that Daniel was given a larger degree of the first gifts mentioned, and there was the release of an unusual mantle. This occurred because of Daniel's great character and faith in God.

If we are going to walk in a higher level with God and expect Him to release us into greater measures of anointing, we have to decide that we will do what it takes to keep our integrity intact. We have to learn not to compromise our standards and beliefs because we fear the consequences. We have so any excuses as to why we are undercover Christians, but we can learn for Daniel and see that strength of character is essential.

BE CONSISTENT

When I was in the nine-to-five workforce, I worked with both believers and nonbelievers. I never kept it a secret that I was a minister, and my coworkers would often ask me for advice. On one such occasion, one of my coworkers made a point to tell me how comfortable they felt coming to me with their concerns because of how consistent I was in my faith in comparison to the other believers on the job. This stuck with me for many years and always reminds me of the importance of not compromising my character regardless of the setting I'm in.

Strong Character Positions You to Receive Rare Gifts

Job 33:23 says, "If there be gift and a messenger with him, an interpreter, one among a thousand, to shew unto man his uprightness" (KJV). This verse points to the rareness of certain gifts. The gift of interpretation is a rare but essential gift. It helps us to know what God is saying through prophecy.

Only two known Bible characters possessed this gift of interpretation—Joseph and Daniel. I believe that this gift was given to these two men because they demonstrated great character and integrity. There is no doubt that Joseph had great character. Genesis 39 chronicles his story and his eventual ascend to a position second in command to the throne. To see a demonstration of the character traits that afforded him his position, I want to take a look at a very specific point in this young man's life.

Near the start of his new life in Egypt after his brothers sold him to a passing caravan, Joseph was placed in charge of everything in the home of the man he was purchased to serve. This man's name was Potiphar, a very wealthy and powerful man.

As Joseph grew and matured, he became a very handsome young man and caught the eye of Potiphar's wife. She wanted him to lay with her, but he refused.

> "Look," he told her, "my master trusts me with everything in his entire household. No one here has more authority than I

> do. He has held back nothing from me except you, because you are his wife. How could I do such a wicked thing? It would be a great sin against God."
>
> —GENESIS 39:8, NLT

Joseph's integrity was tested. He was a young man faced with sexual advancements, and he still chose to respect himself, God, and Potiphar by standing his ground and turning away from sin.

It's easy in this day and age to speak of our weaknesses and allow them to get the best of us. We give our young people excuses to live in ways that bring no honor to them or God. But here we have a young man faced with great opposition, and he was able to withstand the wiles of the enemy.

If we are going to raise up a young generation that is skilled and gifted, we must teach them to walk in integrity and teach them the importance of building character. God was with Joseph even after he was thrown in prison, and he was once again given a high-ranking position:

> But the LORD was with Joseph in the prison and showed him his faithful love. And the LORD made Joseph a favorite with the prison warden. Before long, the warden put Joseph in charge of all the other prisoners and over everything that happened in the prison. The warden had no more worries, because Joseph took care of everything. The LORD was with him and caused everything he did to succeed.
>
> —VV. 21–23, NLT

Joseph was tested and was found faithful to God and His ordinances. He kept himself and because of this he found favor in the sight of God. He was also increased in his gifts to see and interpret the strategies and wisdom of God.

We see so many transgressions in the church today. It's a sad day in the body of Christ when you can't tell the church from the world. When the word of a Christian is no better than the word of a person who serves another god.

The favor of God on Joseph's life was evident. His character allowed him to be in sole charge of Potiphar's house, the prison, and eventually the entire kingdom. The scriptures are clear: they trusted a slave over their own kind. They trusted a slave to operate their administrative affairs. On one hand it was favor, but do you think if they thought Joseph was a swindler or a cheat they would risk their livelihood on the word or honor of a slave? No. His character and integrity made a difference to the level of favor and promotion he received.

CAN GOD TRUST YOU?

I love the way God works. Once He sees that you are trustworthy, He unlocks gifts in you that will catapult you into greater positions. Joseph had one more test of his character ahead of him, probably the most critical: would he tell the truth even if it meant a detrimental outcome to the person?

In prison, Joseph came into contact with two men who needed their dreams interpreted. One man's dream would be favorable, while the other man's dream would take him to the depths of despair. How would Joseph handle interpreting a dream with such a harsh reality? He handled it with wisdom, honesty, and clarity, and left the rest to God.

> "This is what the dream means," Joseph told him. "The three baskets also represent three days. Three days from now Pharaoh will lift you up and impale your body on a pole. Then birds will come and peck away at your flesh."
> —GENESIS 40:18–19, NLT

Can God trust you to tell the truth? Being a truthful person is an important characteristic. Had Joseph lied to the butler to make him feel good, would he then lie to pharaoh, when the pressure was really on? God had to be sure Joseph wielded a strong character. He had to be trusted with many high-ranking task and godly mysteries. He stood the test again and again, placing himself in position to receive from God.

Joseph was greatly rewarded in his spiritual life just as Daniel was with great wisdom and knowledge. They were given the ability to know dreams that had yet to be revealed, to dream dreams, and to interpret them. Daniel and Joseph both exhibited great character and integrity. There was evidence of supernatural spiritual giftings, and they held high-ranking positions to kings and served foreign kingdoms for many years.

May their life be an example to us all and a lesson to strive for excellence in all that we do. When we move into proper alignment with God, may He trust us enough to release positions of prominence and giftings that will not only change the world but also bring glory to the kingdom.

Chapter Seven

HOLY SPIRIT—THE SEER'S GUIDE

H OLY SPIRIT IS a pivotal partner in the seer realm. He is the One who leads us into all knowledge. First Corinthians 2:10 says, "But God hath revealed them unto us by his Spirit: for the Spirit searcheth all things, yea, the deep things of God" (KJV). We need the Holy Spirit when it comes to interpretation because interpretation is a form of parabolic speech or what the Scriptures refer to as a dark saying. If a dream is given to us by God, then only God can reveal it to us. Psalm 78:2 says, "I will open my mouth in a parable: I will utter dark sayings of old."

Parables and darks saying are like riddles that have to be deciphered. They are mysteries from heaven that are not readily known to men. They must be revealed by the Holy Spirit. The Holy Spirit is indispensable when it comes to this gift and cannot be replaced by mere resources. First Corinthians 2:12–13 says, "Now we have received, not the spirit of the world, but the spirit which is of God; that we might know the things that are freely given to us of God. Which things also we speak, not in the words which man's wisdom teacheth, but which the Holy Ghost teacheth; comparing spiritual things with spiritual" (KJV).

SEEKING THE MYSTERIES OF HEAVEN

We need to be in relationship with the Holy Spirit. He is the only One who can understand spiritual things. There can be no substitute for this intimate connection. It is erroneous thinking to believe that God will just give away deep revelations just because we are His children. God wants all to be saved and none to perish, but we have to come into relationship with Him to receive His gift of salvation. Likewise, we cannot be a stranger to God most of the time and expect Him to trust us with His most precious secrets. God is a rewarder of those who diligently seek Him (Heb. 11:6). It is in this seeking of God that we are rewarded with revelation. Proverbs 25:2 states: "It is the glory of God to conceal a matter; to search out a matter is the glory of kings" (NIV).

As we seek to know the mysteries of heaven, we have to pray and seek out the Holy Spirit for His wisdom and guidance in prayer. The Scriptures teach us that He is the One who will make utterance for us when we don't know what to pray (Rom. 8:26). The Holy Spirit has to become our best friend. He is the life companion God left here to help us understand His love language.

Without the Holy Spirit, dreams and visions will seem aloof or far off. We will dismiss them as having no meaning or we will try our hand at interpretation from within our own flesh. This can be dangerous, and we can lead others astray with erroneous revelations. We have to remember that dreams are also prophecy and should be handled with the same care and honor as a spoken word.

IF WE HAVE THE HOLY SPIRIT, DO WE NEED AN INTERPRETER?

When Joseph was in prison, he heard that there were men who needed understanding of his dream. One of the first things Joseph made known he proclaimed to the butler and baker was that the dreams belonged to God. Then he asked them to tell him their dreams. (See Genesis 40:8.)

Joseph understood that he was given a special skill and gift, but he also knew that God wanted to use it for His purposes. With the release of the Holy Spirit, the ability to understand dreams and visions is available to all, but not all possess the skill at a degree as high as perhaps Joseph or Daniel.

In Daniel 9:22, the Bible says, "And he informed me, and talked with me, and said, O Daniel, I am now come forth to give thee skill and understanding" (KJV). Daniel could not decipher the mystery even though the Scriptures tell us he could understand all dreams and all visions. This shows that Daniel had to also be given skill.

There are some dreams that will require an interpreter or even angelic assistance to understand. Interpreters usually possess a higher degree of the gift or a higher skill level in interpretation.

We cannot interpret from our own flesh even with a great dream book and dictionary. We have to first rely on God to give us understanding. We need His Spirit to understand what He is saying. Only the Spirit of God can know the mind of Christ and understand His ways.

INTERACTING WITH THE PRESENCE OF GOD TO RECEIVE REVELATION

When I interpret dreams, I do so in a way that allows room for the Holy Spirit to operate.

1. I keep a consistent prayer life. I love to pray and spend time in the presence of God. I make sure to acknowledge and speak to the Holy Spirit.

2. I ask the Holy Spirit to come close to me. I want the Holy Spirit to feel welcome and to know that I understand my dependence on Him.

3. I ask Him, "What does this dream mean?"

4. I wait and listen for an answer.

This is a template and not to be done routinely, but it will give you a template to learn how to interact with God's presence. Like anything, it takes time and a sincere commitment to meditating on God's Word and a hunger to hear His voice.

LET THE SPIRIT HAVE FULL ACCESS TO YOU

There have been many occasions where I was just about to give an interpretation of a dream and the Spirit corrected me and said, "This is what the dream is saying." I've even been in the middle of an interpretation and He will change my perception of a certain symbol or He will give me the meaning as I am speaking it aloud.

The Holy Spirit needs to have full access to you when you are deciphering dreams. He knows the mind of Christ and His thought toward you. We are just the vessels He speaks through. Never feel bad about the Holy Spirit's correction concerning a dream. Like any gift, there is a margin of error, especially when you are decoding someone else's dream.

The most important key to remember is that we have to be open to the leading of God's Spirit at all times and be mindful of our own fallibility. The Holy Spirit brings a clarity that cannot be dismissed, and without His powerful insight and presence, we would find accurate dream interpretation impossible to achieve.

Chapter Eight

A PROPHET, NOT A PSYCHIC

THE BIBLE SAYS that false prophets have been released among us. As you should know, the answer to the false prophet, witch, necromancer, and psychic is the seer prophet. The Lord opened up the seer realm for this very reason.

For me, growing up in the church included facing a lot of issues. Often, people would say I was making things up when I would exercise my gifts. They couldn't understand how I could see certain things or interpret dreams and visions.

There are those who do not understand the difference between a psychic and a prophet. I would get a vision or have a dream, and people would try to tell me I was performing witchcraft. In this very time that we live in, people don't believe that the seer realm is of God. After encountering such individuals who are concerned about the biblical and spiritual validity of the seer gifts and those who had never seen them in operation, I became convinced that there is a great need for clarity about this what this realm is and is not. In this chapter, I will break down the difference between the authentic prophetic-seer realm and its counterfeits.

I have seen so many people broken, hurt, and abused in church, because they were told their gift was demonic. Can you image the confusion this would cause a believer? There have been many believers who have turned to the psychic world because of these types of erroneous teachings. Let me start by saying: Surprise!

You are in fact operating within the bounds of a supernatural God, no matter what you have been told. You are not demonic. You are not talking to the dead. You are not inviting familiar spirits. You are walking with God.

When I first started out operating as a seer, one of my family members, who had not been exposed to the seer gift, asked me, "Are you like a psychic?"

I was shocked: "What? No, I'm not a psychic!"

The issue is that the only contact they had with a person who could see supernaturally was a psychic. This is an alarming, especially when there are many in the body of Christ who operate in this particular realm. We have to understand that some people do not actually know the difference between psychics and prophets. A lot of people are just confused. The seer gift does not garner enough attention in the church and many leaders are not discussing it.

The seer realm is used by both psychics and prophets, so there are similarities in the function, but the operation is completely different. There are godly things other people have seen witches perform, and because of this deceptive crossover, we must undertake this discussion as believers. If there is an original, you will surely be introduced to the counterfeit. Uncertainty in the church world will inevitably cause needless persecution to God's prophets.

What is the difference between psychics and prophets? The difference is very simple. A seer prophet has his radar tuned in to God's signal and operates under the authority of heaven. A psychic sees and operates under demonic control and influence. In other words, prophets hear from God and witches and psychics hear from demons. They hear from demonic and familiar spirits. They speak to them and talk to them.

Those who work in witchcraft can travel through supernatural planes, and in Scripture prophets also travel with the leading of God through the spirit realm. We know that witches cast spells and do incantations. In one of the later chapters, I will discuss how they astral travel by willing themselves out of their bodies. They use demonic influences to do things for them. They send demons out to do their bidding. They work with the demonic realm to enforce the enemy's plans.

Witches and psychics spend hours in demonic temples performing blood sacrifices and taking blood oaths. This all is very real. God expressly forbid these types of interactions. Leviticus 20:6 says, "If a person turns to mediums and necromancers, whoring after them, I will set my face against that person and will cut him off from among his people." Basically, if you are not engaging the spiritual realm from a biblical perspective, you are doing it the wrong way.

In my experience, I know first-hand that people are perplexed about how these gifts can function from a biblical perspective. I've had conversations with some, and after telling them that I am a seer who operates in dreams and visions, they tell me about a loved one who operates within the same realm of gifts. Initially, it seems the same, but as I probe deeper into what they mean, the more I realize they don't mean that their loved one is prophetic in the biblical sense. They mean that they were using witchcraft.

I've been told about loved ones whose spirits traveled to places and or who talked to spirits at will. In one situation, a woman told me about her mother who engaged in this realm. When we got to the part about her visions, it became clear that her mother was practicing witchcraft. Since she had recently given her life to Christ, I helped to her understand the difference between demonic influence and godly sight. Then we prayed together for her sight to be cleansed, so she could walk in freedom with her seer gift. God had given this woman a precious gift, but it was unfortunately tainted by the witchcraft practiced by her family.

If someone who understands the differences between the demonic and biblical expressions in the seer realm isn't there to retrieve these precious gifts, we can lose them to the occult. Let me be clear: not everyone who has the gift of sight is a prophet. Some are able to operate because of the illegal access gained through the occult. Once you pray for demonic doors to be closed in their lives, some will either retain a purified version of their gift or lose it completely.

MIXTURES IN THE BODY OF CHRIST

Mixtures between the demonic and the holy are becoming commonplace in our churches, because we won't teach on the seer realm. Some people come in to the church from certain cultural backgrounds where occult practices are the norm, especially religious practices involving demonic activity. We need to be able to instruct these precious ones with understanding and help them know the right way to access the mysteries of the Spirit of God. They need guidance to know what to do with their gifts of sight, but they have not yet been cleansed.

Some of the evidence I have disclosed to these new believers is that they are still influenced by the demonic is that they've retained the ability to leave their bodies at will, they still experience dark visions, and they can still speak with the dead. These are common occurrences for those with backgrounds and cultures whose religious experiences are mixed with the occult. Without the proper counsel and loving guidance, some people take a little bit of what they use to do such as dabbling in crystals or other forms of witchcraft, and mix it into their Christianity, instead of completely eradicating the behavior.

While working for a summer camp, I ran into a young lady who was a Christian. We began to have conversations about God and our particular giftings. One day she asked me if I would pray for her. I agreed, but I had not told her I was a prophet. While I prayed for her, I clearly heard the word *witchcraft*. I asked her about it after the prayer. She seemed a bit puzzled and denied any wrongdoing. I probed further, explaining that the witchcraft I saw was in her family line and still very much alive. She reluctantly told me that her mother used to be heavily into crystals, she used to hang them around her room when she was younger.

She went on to explain that she had been going to see a Christian crystal healer. This shocked me. I had never heard of this practice. She said people usually have a hard time with what she does, so she doesn't speak of it often. The enemy loves darkness and likes to keep his deeds secret. I began to share with her the error in the teaching of the crystals, and how God is the only one we need to make us clean.

This woman's story is an example for why we need to teach the seer realm and not be afraid of it. Light and darkness cannot dwell together, and as Ephesians 5:8, says, we were once darkness, now we are light in the Lord. We should walk as children of light.

You cannot be a Christian witch. It is not possible. Light and darkness have nothing to do with each other. We must begin to expel the mixtures in the church.

Yoga

I want to talk a little about yoga. Yoga is a form of exercise that many people are embracing. Looking at the root of yoga, you will find the reason for certain poses and meditations. Yoga was a practice that has roots in religious practices by those who do not believe in God. Practicing an art form without true understanding can really cause you problems.

We must always be sure to look behind the scenes of certain things and weigh the cost. The devil is crafty. He is not going to just bring things to us right in our face. He tries to slide it in and make it acceptable. You will have people coming to you telling you can do many things, but you must make sure you submit everything to God in prayer.

Chrislim

Something that I hear all the time that really bothers me is Christians who are always trying to look for the new next "big" thing. You have to be careful when looking for the next thing. Ask yourself, "Is it good or is it God?" Some things are just not going to be God. As you seek these things, consider who or what you are talking to and what you are meditating on. You cannot be Buddhist, Christian, and Muslim all at the same time.

I began to hear the term "Chrislim." It is a mixture of Christianity and the Muslim faith. There has been quite a push in recent years to merge these two groups together. Most unsuspecting Christians will fall for this merger because of a couple reasons: 1) many are not versed in the differences between the religions, and 2) tolerance. The Bible says, "My people perish for a lack of knowledge" (Hosea 4:6). You need to know the truth of God's Word to know when something false presents itself. Otherwise, you may find yourself deceived.

We cannot afford to follow trendy patterns. The Bible is clear that there is only one clear path to the Father and that is Jesus Christ. You cannot mix all religions together and call yourself a Christian.

Books

Because I interpret dreams, many people who come to me about the dreams they have, and during our interactions they ask questions about different books they are reading. Books such as Book of Enoch and other literature that may have questionable roots seem to come up a lot. Some are asking why these books are not in the Bible and are studying them as if they are valid information. I let them know that these books are opening doors for demonic influence and they are confusing themselves by reading them without understanding their context and relationship to the Scriptures.

Many of us don't know enough about our own faith to

adequately weigh the truth and error in these other books. We are not solid in what we understand about the Bible and about what God has actually spoken.

So, yes, some of these are books were written during the times that certain portions of Scripture were written, but they were not placed in the Bible because they were either heretical or could not be authenticated against the ancient Hebrew scrolls and Greek manuscripts written by the prophets and apostles. Above all, they were not supernaturally confirmed by the Spirit of God. He watches over His Word. The books of the Bible as we have them now were accepted by the church centuries ago. I encourage you to study how the Bible came to be so that you can know this for yourself. You can begin your studies at BlueLetterBible.org with the article titled "The Canon of Scripture."[1] The link for this study is in the Notes section of this book.

Our lack of knowledge in this area will cause us to be easy prey for the enemy when we hear about the possibility of "lost books" or that the Holy Bible is incomplete or full of mistakes. It is important to stand confidently in these days knowing that we have the full and complete Bible as God intended it. If we can't trust God's Word, how will we stand against the falsehoods that threaten us, our families, and our communities?

Now when it comes to religious books from other faith traditions, think about it this way: when you are trying to convince someone to come to Christ, one of the strategies you may use is to make reference to a source the person may already understand. For example, if I am talking to a Muslim and I'm trying to bring them over to Christianity, I am going to say, "Your Quran mentions this" or "In your Quran, it even says that Jesus Christ did the only miracles." As I speak to this person, I'm going to reference something they are already familiar with. This will allow the hearer to have a clear point of reference because this is a source that they trust and have confidence in. This is often done to bridge the gap in their understanding thus allowing them to be more in tune with what is being presented.

This can happen the other way around as well. For instance, if a Jehovah's Witness is trying to evangelize a Christian, they will mention things from the Holy Bible that are also part of their religious book and faith tradition. They do this to draw a connection.

So, just because another religious book refers to something that is also mentioned in the Bible doesn't mean the other religious book expresses the authoritative and inerrant word of God. When we as believers discuss these books with a person of a different faith, it should only be used with the hope of connecting with that person and expanding their thinking into the true things of God. So, yes, someone may mention a certain book, but that does not mean that book is a one Christians should read as a biblical source or supplement.

Everything must be studied in context in order to get the clearest view of what God is conveying. You have to understand why things are mentioned and why things are being said. We have to get rid of some of this stuff. Get rid of some of these ideologies out here.

Another example I want to share about books that introduce mixed elements has to do with something that happened to me when I was in college. To this day, I think it is interesting. In one of my psychology classes, we studied Carl Jung and Sigmund Freud. Jung wrote a book called *The Seven Sermons to the Dead*. By the way, these men would take cocaine and get high. Jung's book was all about how he would talk to demons. Demons would come out of the pictures he had in his office. He would have conversations with them and write down what he was told. There is even one psychological attribute derived from Carl Jung that developed out of his encounters that was just like the demonic entity he frequented.

Through this example, we can see that there may be problems

with the demonic crossing over into certain fields of study, we don't realize how they intertwine the demonic into our daily lives. As we set out into or individual fields of study. Principles we learn in our pursuit of higher education sometimes have their roots firmly grounded in occult practices.

The demonology that we see here is also coming into the church because we don't question things. Just like we don't question the aunt who goes into the back room we are not allowed to go into, and when she emerges with ointments or medicine and tells us to take it, we do it without question. And just like that, we could have just participated in witchcraft unknowingly.

Let's pray for wisdom and discernment is it needed for today.

INFORMATION VS. REVELATION

Next, we have to deal with those who are moved by the "accuracy" of these psychics. Accuracy is not a test to see if a spirit is of God, we know this because in Acts 16:16–18, it says,

> It happened that as we were going to the place of prayer, a slave-girl having a spirit of divination met us, who was bringing her masters much profit by fortune-telling. Following after Paul and us, she kept crying out, saying, "These men are bond-servants of the Most High God, who are proclaiming to you the way of salvation." She continued doing this for many days. But Paul was greatly annoyed, and turned and said to the spirit, "I command you in the name of Jesus Christ to come out of her!" And it came out at that very moment.
>
> —NASB

This woman spoke with accuracy when shouting information concerning these disciples, but when Paul grew weary of her, he cast the spirit out. The Bible tells us we have to test the spirit by the Spirit. What does that mean? Simply put, what you are hearing and receiving has to line up with God's Word. God's Word is living, breathing, and, by its very nature, revelatory.

Most psychics deal with information about past things or events. If you are working with familiar spirits, you are not a prophet. God calls prophets from birth; therefore, you may have started off as a prophet but right now you are operating in a spirit that is not of God. God's power is far superior to that of the occult, whether or not you find some accuracy in what is practiced.

In looking at the lives of Moses and Aaron, do you remember the time when they were sent to pharaoh on assignment to let the children of Israel free from their bondage and the pharaoh's magicians Egypt imitated the miracle when Aaron's rod turned into a serpent? The magicians were able to execute the same act. However, the rod serpent that Aaron threw down ate up all of theirs. (See Exodus 7:10–12.) This shows you that, while the devil can imitate the look of some supernatural happenings, God's power is far greater than that of the demonic world.

Identifying False Prophets

How do you spot false prophets, witches, and others who are involved in occult activity? We really need to pray for a spirit of discernment, which is the divine ability to rightly judge what is going on. In its broadest sense, discernment is closely related to wisdom as an expression of the Spirit of God. By this Spirit, we can function in the manner that Jesus did: "He shall not judge after the sight of his eyes, neither reprove after the hearing of his ears" (Isa. 11:2). God gives us a measure of discernment and it is further developed through study of the Scriptures. But there is also what we call "discerning of spirits," which is needed to judge between your spirit, God's Spirit, or Satan's. It is a spiritual gift imparted by the Holy Spirit (1 Cor. 12:10). It is also closely related to wisdom, but it is somewhat different in that it involves specific knowledge given supernaturally.

The gift of discernment is lacking in the body. With discernment, you can spot false prophets and those who don't bring you truth. Discernment will help you recognize when what they say doesn't line up with the Word or voice of God. I'm going to stress again: you need discernment, because the enemy is crafty. You are going to have a hard time, if you don't have discernment and wisdom.

A few years ago, a show came out called *Psychic Kids*. I watched it one day while I was bored at home. The show features kids with special gifts. Some could speak to the dead or see into the supernatural realm. I watched as these psychics traveled around to "help" the kids with their gifts. For the most part, they had the kids believing they were psychics or mediums. My heart hurt so much for these children, and once again I had to ask, "Where was the church?"

DRAWING IN THOSE WHO OPERATE IN WITCHCRAFT BUT SHOULD BE PROPHETS

If there are people who are actually out there practicing witchcraft but should have been prophets, how do we bring them into the kingdom? First, we have to witness to them. That's right. We have to get outside the walls of the church. We cannot be scared to go to those who are in the occult. They are looking and searching for the same thing as we are—the truth. They possess a gift of sight but have no clue what to do with it. The world is presenting to them what they should do with it, while the church unwittingly stays silent. We stay silent while the world woos them with a false purpose.

The church has to present the truth to the world, but we are fearful of the unknown. We are scared of witches. We are scared that they are going to curse us, even though the Bible tells us we have more power than the enemy. The church has to understand and know its authority. We have more power, light, understanding, truth, and protection than anything the enemy can muster. We have to go out and begin to really open up about this realm. This realm is very important and is not taught enough in the church. The seer realm is biblical, and you can find so much evidence for it in Scripture, especially in the books of Acts and Revelations.

There is something I want you to understand. There are people out there in the occult (not all but some) who have practiced witchcraft and consorted with demons and had no way of knowing that they were called to be prophets. When I was in college, there was a lady who was over our dorm. She was not a practicing witch. When I met her, she had come into Christianity and she had a very strong prophetic gift of sight (seer). She did believe that some of it was stronger because she had been in witchcraft. She didn't believed that once you opened certain doors they never fully close all the way. She found out that she was really a prophet.

During her time as a witch people were always trying to call her out of it, but she believed that witchcraft and Christianity could go together. She had always had the gift of sight but was not raised in the church. She decided that she was going to go, become a full witch, and join a coven. Before talking the last steps, she ended up praying because some Christian friends had been talking to her about it, telling her, "You know, you can't do that."

Her story is really an awesome testimony of how God blocked her from being in coven and solidifying her commitment to it. When she came out of that world she was still able to see a lot of things—things she should not be able to because she used to do spells, stand in salt circles, and do incantations (channeling spirts). She really thought she could be a "good" witch, what she called a "white witch." She wasn't into "black" magic (even though it's all dark).

She told me that she would stand in a salt circle naked, because that was supposed to keep the demons from coming into the circle with her while she channeled. Well, one day, she started recognizing that there were books that would show up in her house that she didn't remember buying on black magic. Demons would be in the house and that scared her because the salt circle was supposed to keep them away. She didn't know how they were still there because she told them to go. She was doing all this because she thought she could be a "good" witch.

The Lord saved her out of that lifestyle. She learned a lot being in that world. For one, it's all a lie. There is no such thing as a "good" witch. The devil came in and deceived her. She was under a very strong delusion to the point that she was drawing a mural on her wall that she thought was a very beautiful, gorgeous mural, until God opened up her spiritual eyes. When He did, she saw that she was drawing some type of blood-looking, crazy pattern on the wall.

She thanks God every day that her friends were not afraid to go to her and tell her, "You are not a witch. Come out of that lifestyle." When she came out of that lifestyle and her gift was cleansed, she realized she was a prophet of the Lord. She has since done great things for the Lord.

There are people who operate in the occult with no recourse and no hope, because they don't know what they actually had was a prophetic gift and not a demonic one.

WHEN PROPHETS ATTRACT WITCHES

I have been asked why prophets attract witches. I don't think that they attract them necessarily, but I do believe the supernatural is attracted to the supernatural. Anytime you have the truth, you are going to be challenged with what is false, because the enemy wants to bring reproach upon God's people.

In the life of a prophet who is truly of God and speaks the truth, the enemy is going to bring a counterfeit in to discredit that prophet. You may hear people say, "All prophets are this," "All prophets want money," "All prophets are liars." What they've have done by speaking these generalizations is brought in another spirit to discredit the prophet and the prophetic realm. The devil doesn't want the prophet to go forth and bring truth to the church.

If the enemy can operate in the supernatural realm, how much greater would the children of God be if we operated in the spiritual realm? The Spirit of God is greater than anything. If we could ever get a hold of our seer gift, our visionary gift, our dream gift, and start operating authentically, we would be a force to reckon with. So of course the enemy is coming to tear it down. Some of the ways he does that is by calling the prophets of God liars and witches, and saying they are not of God. He wants us to lose courage and confidence in our gifts. If he can get us to despise our gifts, he knows that he can cause them to go dormant.

The enemy wants to shut your gift down. He wants to silence you. He doesn't want you traveling in the spirit and speaking blessing over your regions. He does not want you to do these things. The enemy really doesn't want you saving people at all. He does not want God's power to be shown.

We see this in our churches around the globe. The power of God is not being shown strong in our churches, because the church is so far away for the original plan. We are supposed to be performing greater works than what Jesus did. Why are we not operating at this level? Because we have allowed a lot of corruption to seep into the church. This is not to bash the church. It's just that we need to arise and fight to redeem the things we have lost. Things have happened unwittingly, yes, but we should not be content to continue with such ignorance and apathy.

One thing that we do that we have to be careful of is taking principles of the world and trying to bring them into our churches. Instead, we should be taking principles of the church and releasing them into the world. We will spend a lot time doing the opposite. I'm not against sound business ideas and strategies, but they should not be ruling our churches.

God has given the church greater insight through the revelatory gifts as well as the prophetic. We should be using these gifts as a means to lead instead of follow. There is a woman I encountered some time ago. She was working in the beauty industry. She had horribly cracked skin on her hands due to the chemicals she used. She began to pray about her hands because she had found no solution to the problem. One night, she had a dream in which she was given the ingredients to make a hand cream. She used this product on her hands and watched as her skin was rejuvenated. She now markets and sells this product. God can give us witty ideas and inventions. He can give us cutting-edge ideas. We just have to push into this realm.

People no longer rely on the Spirit or presence of God. They have become numb to it. Entertainment has taken over for the presence of God. We don't clamor for those who tell us the truth, bring correction, and minister the pure word of God. Instead, we clamor for entertainment, to clap our hands, and to feel good when we leave church.

We must cry out and ask God to change our desires. We can't keep compromising in the church. When you compromise in the church, you will teach a watered-down gospel. If we can't bring the truth and light back into our churches, we are not going to be able to see the full demonstration of the power of God. We have to commit to praying once again. We have to make our lifestyle full of worship. We must live a true lifestyle sold out to God. We have to get back to the basic fundamentals of the Word of God. When we do, we will be a force to reckon with.

Chapter Nine

REALMS OF THE SPIRIT

DREAMS, VISIONS, TRANCE, and spiritual travel play a major role in the seer's life and is the primary way in which they interact with God. They rely heavily on their senses and the way they feel. Taste, touch, and smells are important factors in their interaction. These interactions can seem real or literal. They spend a lot of time interpreting encounters and their dependence on the Holy Spirit is significant.

In 2 Corinthians 12:3, Apostle Paul recalls an encounter where he was caught up into a divine vision with God. He said, "And I know that this man was caught up into paradise—whether in the body or out of the body I do not know, God knows."

As a seer, there will be times that the encounters are so real that you will awake not knowing if you were there or not. One such experience happened to me. During a fast, I was praying about portals. That night, I had a dream where I took flight, and the Lord showed me several different regions. I could literally feel the wind in my face, the intense blue of the water, and the sheer magnitude of the buildings took my breath away. Upon awaking, I thought it was a dream, until I looked those images up and found the actual locations causing me to wonder if I had traveled there.

There are other occasions where I have traveled in the spirit. One such occasion came when my parents were on their way to Jamaica. I was really concerned about their hotel accommodations, because the year before, they had had some misfortune. I was praying for them prior to falling asleep. I had a vision in which I was standing at a hotel. I could see the palm trees and could feel the cool air blowing. I could walk up the steps to this hotel and look inside.

When I woke from my slumber, I called my mom and recounted the details of my vision. She sent me a picture, and the resort they were staying in had the exact detail I described, right down to the entrance. It was amazing! I had literally stood on the steps of their resort. God can do amazing things when we take Him out of the box.

SEERS AND ANGELS

One main characteristic of a seer prophet is their ability to see and work with angelic beings. The seer has the ability to see angels, demons, and various other heavenly beings. Ezekiel often had visions of these types of beings and interacted with them to get answers to dreams or visions he did not understand. His most famous passage in Scripture deals with a vision of a wheel.

> Now as I looked at the living beings, behold, there was one wheel on the earth beside the living beings, for each of the four of them. The appearance of the wheels and their workmanship was like sparkling beryl, and all four of them had the same form, their appearance and workmanship being as if one wheel were within another. Whenever they moved, they moved in any of their four directions without turning as they moved.
> —EZEKIEL 1:15–17

The seer will have varying degrees of encounters with the supernatural realm. Depending on the type of prophet you are and your assignment to the kingdom. The magnitude of your encounters may also vary depending on your specific season.

I wish I could say my first encounter with supernatural beings was with angels, but I was not that lucky. In my first experiences, I would see demons, and initially, I was terrified of them. These encounters caused me a lot of issues with fear, which the enemy uses to attack the seer early in life. The reasons we encounter the demonic world can vary. I found out that two of my giftings were healing and deliverance. I would see demons in my dreams as well as physically attached to people. Seeing these demonic beings, though disconcerting, ended up being a lesson in spiritual warfare.

One such occasion, I dreamed I was trapped in my bedroom by these demonic spirits. They were in shadow form and coming in my room under the door. So, I opened up the door and I ran out of the house. When I ran outside, it was nighttime, and I was scared because it was dark outside. Only the street lamps were on. The demons where chasing me, and I ran into an alley, which was a dead end, so I turned around. They were there waiting for me. As I called on the name of Jesus, these spirits' eyes turned into cartoon characters' eyes and they came out of their heads. Then they ran away so fast.

Through this, I know the Lord was teaching me how to fight and to have no fear. I learned the power a believer possesses over these beings, and our authority with these creatures of the night.

Seers rely heavily on the supernatural realm. They will work with and are sometimes assigned certain types of angels. Angels can bring different types of miracles, healings, or blessings into an atmosphere. Many seers operate in response to their presence. It is not strange to hear a seer proclaim during services that they can see an angel and what that angel is doing, wearing, or the type of gift they are releasing into atmosphere. Some seers will not operate in a service until their assigned angel shows up. This is not the case for all seers, but it is becoming increasingly common as we learn more about the gift and how it is intended function.

> Then Elisha prayed and said, "O LORD, I pray, open his eyes that he may see." And the LORD opened the servant's eyes and he saw; and behold, the mountain was full of horses and chariots of fire all around Elisha. When they came down to him, Elisha prayed to the LORD and said, "Strike this people with blindness, I pray." So, He struck them with blindness according to the word of Elisha.
> —2 KINGS 6:17–18, KJV

In this passage, you can see that Elisha was surrounded by the host of heaven who were there to help Elisha defeat the Syrians. The angelic host often works with the seer to advance God's objectives.

THE SEER AND THE GLORY REALM OF GOD

The seer often operates in the glory realm of God and can detect its presence, because they have a special sensitivity to the supernatural realm. Seers can often see and reveal the operation of the Spirit. There are multiple accounts of seeing dark clouds show up in service, depicting the glory of God in a room. They will see signs of supernatural oil or visions of Jesus standing nearby. They have even spotted supernatural body parts that hover over a person who is asking for a healing.

A high level of worship follows most seers as they are carriers of God's presence. His presence will often be marked by visions of open heavens, where His glory is shown forth. Let's look at an example of this through a story from the life of Stephen the deacon.

In Acts 6, there is narrative that tells us of a great man named Stephen who had done great wonders and miracles. He was to suffer great persecution and, later, we would see that this persecution was even unto death. However, Stephen was full of the wisdom of God and was defending himself against those who lied against him. Before he was taken from this world, he looked up and saw Jesus standing on the right hand of the Father:

> Being full of the Holy Ghost, looked up steadfastly into heaven, and saw the glory of God, and Jesus standing on the right hand of God.
> —ACTS 6:55

We can see here that visions will bring us comfort as well as display the glory and majesty of God. Stephen was allowed a glimpse into heaven and given a front-row seat to see the glory of God on display.

Throughout Scripture, we can see where the heavens opened, and a glorious appearing of the Lord was captured. Many would even say that this signifies an open heaven. In Genesis 28:10–17, Jacob saw angels ascending and descending a stairway. Then the Lord proclaimed that the land he was on was given to him and his descendants. When Jacob arose, he thought surely God was in this place and he did not perceive it.

God will use this realm to show us where an open heaven or a place of blessing lies (sometimes referred to as portals). More importantly, He will tell us where we belong. To see how this is true, we can turn to the prophet Isaiah. He had a particular experience with God's glory:

> In the year that king Uzziah died I saw also the Lord sitting upon a throne, high and lifted up, and his train filled the temple.
> —ISAIAH 6:1, KJV

Isaiah had and open vision, where he experienced, with his natural eye, a vision of God. He looked into an open heaven, and he was allowed to peer through the thin veil that separates the natural from the supernatural.

THE SEER AND TRAVELING THE REALMS OF THE SPIRIT

As I delved deeper into this realm, I realized the opportunities for interacting with a supernatural God are limitless. What if you could do more than just see in the spirit? What if you could see the place you would go or live? What if God allowed you to travel in your dreams? Ezekiel 8:3 states:

> He stretched out the form of a hand and caught me by a lock of my head; and the Spirit lifted me up between earth and heaven and brought me in the visions of God to Jerusalem, to the entrance of the north gate of the inner court, where the seat of the idol of jealousy, which provokes to jealousy, was located.
>
> —NASB

For the prophet, traveling in dreams could be to a specific natural location or it could be as it was for Paul. He traveled to a heavenly location in 2 Corinthians 12:2.

It is this ability to not only see what God is doing in your dreams but also to travel that makes dreams and visions such an important part of the prophetic. God showed Ezekiel the landscape and took him to the place of Israel's the transgression. However, Paul was speaking of a different location, not a physical place on earth, but of being caught up to the third heavens, traveling from one position on the earth to supernatural position in the heavenlies.

The visionary realm holds many mysteries that we need as the body of Christ. We are not taking advantage of our position as believers.

Natural travel

There is also a natural travel that some have experienced. Phillip experienced this after his encounter with an Ethiopian eunuch:

> And he commanded the chariot to stop, and they both went down into the water, Philip and the eunuch, and he baptized him. And when they came up out of the water, the Spirit of the Lord carried Philip away, and the eunuch saw him no more, and went on his way rejoicing. But Philip found himself at Azotus, and as he passed through he preached the gospel to all the towns until he came to Caesarea.
> —Acts 8:38–40

Phillip was literally moved, by the hand of God to another city, so that he could continue preaching the gospel of salvation to the lost. There are no limitations in the seer realm, God can do what he wants, by His power and authority.

The Seer's Senses While Caught in the Spirit

I love the fact that all of our senses function in the seer realm. Ezekiel was able to use all of his natural senses while being caught up in his vision. Ezekiel 3:3 says, "And he said unto me, Son of man, cause thy belly to eat, and fill thy bowels with this roll that I give thee. Then did I eat it; and it was in my mouth as honey for sweetness" (KJV).

In this great vision, Ezekiel was ordered to eat, and while in this state he could even taste the sweetness of the scroll and sense the bitter feeling it left in his stomach.

Seer's can taste, touch and smell in this realm. There have been times that my dreams are so real that I wake up chewing. Seers can smell pungent or sweet smells and even feel the presence of the substance they are interacting with. The seer realm is a wide-open book waiting for us to delve into and experience.

The Seer and Trances

Another state in which the seer operates in is what we call a trance. The word comes from the Greek word *ekstasis*, where our

English word *ecstasy* comes from. It is the state of a person being "out of himself."[1] In Acts 10:9–10, we see that Peter had such an experience.

> On the morrow, as they went on their journey, and drew nigh unto the city, Peter went up upon the housetop to pray about the sixth hour: and he became very hungry, and would have eaten: but while they made ready, he fell into a trance.
>
> —KJV

Peter was waiting for his supper and never left his location. He was simply outside of himself and having this great vision. He was waiting for his food, when God pulled him into a vision of unclean animals descending. When you are open to God, He can invade your natural with His supernatural at any time.

On another occasion, in Act 22:17, Paul was pulled into a trance during prayer: "And it came to pass, that, when I was come again to Jerusalem, even while I prayed in the temple, I was in a trance" (KJV).

Trances in Peter's and Paul's cases are called "a preternatural, absorbed state of mind preparing for the reception of the vision."[2] In each instance, they were being prepared to receive a vision from the Lord. Strong prayer warriors will often experience these states as well. Prayer and meditation will also bring you into these types of states to receive visions from God.

Trance states can also mean "astonishment" or "amazed." We see one such example of this in Ezekiel 3:15:

> So the Spirit lifted me up and took me away; and I went embittered in the rage of my spirit, and the hand of the LORD was strong on me. Then I came to them of the captivity at Telabib, that dwelt by the river of Chebar, and I sat where they sat, and remained there astonished among them seven days.
>
> —KJV

He was literally in this state of amazement for seven days, awaiting the word of the Lord. Here we can see that these states can last for differing periods of time.

The visionary realm uses all our senses to bring us into a full revelation of what the Lord has to say to us. Dreams and visions help us experience the fullness of who God is. He moves us to understanding by using this very realm to cause us to wonder if we are in the body or out. He will use this realm to fill us with His awe and wonder. He will show us the truth and allow us to experience things we could not on our own. God uses dreams and visions to take us beyond our human limitations and progress us into dimension where there are no limits.

We need to learn and understand these realms of the spirit, for in these days the spirit of God is only going to get stronger and the manifestations greater. In the very least we need to be ready and open to true God encounters.

Chapter Ten

HOW TO RESPOND TO YOUR DREAMS AND VISIONS

OFTEN PEOPLE HAVE dreams and visions and do not know what to do with them. They try to pray to get some understanding but still do not know what the Lord wants them to do. After you have a dream or vision and the Lord does give an interpretation, you must then ask God to give you strategy so that you can respond appropriately.

In Genesis 41, we read about a troubling dream Pharaoh had. The dream was sent as a warning to him about what was about to happen in the land. Not having the Spirit of God, Pharaoh called for Joseph who had the gift of dream interpretation. Like Pharaoh, many of us have dreams and visions but we have no understanding of them. If we cannot understand or interpret the dreams God gives us, then we need to pray and ask God for revelation. Or we can ask someone we know who is gifted in dream interpretation to help us discover its meaning. It's also important that we learn, to some degree, how to interpret our own dreams.

Dreams are prophecies expressed through visual images, as if through a movie lens. They are words displayed as images delivered to us to bring about change in our lives. Through dreams and visions, God will speak to us about our nations, countries, families, churches, and many other things that may concern us.

SEEK INTERPRETATION

Pharaoh did not wait to see what meaning his dream would bring. He immediately asked for an interpreter to tell him what it meant. Like Pharaoh, you need to seek interpretation and work at getting an understanding of the dreams and visions the Lord brings to you. Here are the steps you should follow to receive interpretation of your dreams:

1. Study the Word of God.
2. Pray and ask God for revelation, wisdom, and insight.
3. Seek someone with a credible/confirmed gift of dream interpretation.

We have to treat our dreams like they are important to us. Being good stewards over our dream lives, releases revelation about our dreams.

BUILD A STRATEGY

Once Joseph interpreted Pharaoh's dream, they were left with a situation that needed a solution. They may have thought, "What do we do now that we have understanding?" Joseph immediately went into giving Pharaoh a strategy to save Egypt from the famine.

After the meaning of our dreams is revealed, we must take action. For many of us, this is the hard and potentially harmful part. There have been so many missed opportunities because people failed to act on a prophetic dream. I remember one such case, where I interpreted a dream for this young lady. It was a warning to her to let go of a relationship with a young man. The Lord specifically said that they would lose everything they owned if they did not break off the relationship. The young lady did not heed the warning and found herself in dire straits. She lost everything—her home, car, finances, and even some of her family relationships. When she finally acted, the Lord allowed her to regain all that was lost, but it was a hard lesson—one that could have been avoided. That's why it's important to heed the warnings given through dreams.

Joseph knew the severity of Pharaoh's dream and took action. He gave Pharaoh a strategy that could be implemented before the famine came. He explained what they needed to do: divide the wheat during years of plenty and put some away. That way, they could release it back to the people during the years of famine. He told them how to fix their problem.

Once you realize your dream requires a solution, pray and ask God for wisdom and strategy. In most cases, your dreams are going to require some action. Maybe not one you can readily implement, but you need to begin to prepare yourself and family for change. Joseph did not wait until the famine was upon them, they acted immediately to avoid a future disaster.

Some people want God to give them great big revelatory dreams. They even desire for God to take them up to the heavenlies, but they should ask themselves, "Am I going to act to further the kingdom of God? Am I going to use this gift to bring glory to His name? Or, will I only use it as just an opportunity to boast about my gift?"

TAKE ACTION

God wants His people to take action to further His purposes. Habakkuk 2:1 states:

> I will stand on my guard post and station myself on the rampart; and I will keep watch to see what He will speak to me, and how I may reply when I am reproved. Then the Lord answered me and said, "Record the vision and inscribe it on tablets, that the one who reads it may run."
>
> —NASB

Habakkuk understood how to wait for God to speak and for the instruction that would follow. He was instructed to write the vision down. The simple act of writing the proper information was crucial to God. It was about getting the vision right so there was clarity. How many times have you bothered to write the vision God placed before you?

Joseph's ability to take action coupled with other factors caused him to be promoted. How has your inability to move on your dreams and visions caused you to miss opportunities? People may never know the greatness God has down on the inside of you, because you took your dreams for granted. Some people do not realize that prophecy does not come to pass by osmosis. It's important to pray, "Lord, show me how to respond to this dream. How do I fix this problem? How do I stop this from happening to my nation, my family, and so on? What is it that You would have me to do?"

Visions are usually literal. Dreams are more symbolic. Which means that visions are more likely to come about the way you see them. What if you get a vision that concerns you? Sometimes you don't know why God choose you to share this information with. However, there is a proper response before going to that person about your vision. It always begins with prayer. You have to ask God, "What do I do next with this information? Why did You show this to me, God? Do You want me to intercede? Should I talk to the person?" Ask God to reveal to you why He gave the vision to you.

God is not always asking you to physically go to that person. Sometimes He just wants you to pray. He may be preparing you for what is coming and telling a person about your vision can be harmful to their process.

What if God comes to you and shows you that the nation is going to be crippled? Before you go and start proclaiming the nation's demise, ask Him what He needs you to do about it. He may say, "Call a forty-eight-hour prayer for the nation." He could give you many instructions.

Far too often when the prophets of God received visions or words of prophecy, there was not much action involved other than talking about it. If Joseph would have stopped at the interpretation and did nothing but allow the famine to take place, people would have died.

In Genesis 18, Abraham pleaded with God not to allow Sodom to be destroyed. Abraham was given key information about the fate of many people. He did not fail to act. He petitioned the Lord to have mercy on the people and spare the city. As prophets and seers, we do not have to stand by and watch calamity befall the nation.

OBEDIENCE TO THE WORD OF THE LORD PAYS OFF

I was married only a short time, less than a year. There was so much going on, and I was ready to give up on my marriage. The Lord spoke to me about my husband and told me not to give up. He told me to write him love letters for thirty days and He would turn my marriage around. The Lord said, "No matter what's going or how you feel, write the letters."

For thirty days, I wrote love letters to my husband based on scriptures about God's love for me. I was instructed to express only what I was willing to give for my marriage. I was never to ask for any change from my spouse. It was a hard in the beginning, but I was obedient to the process. Thirty days later, my marriage had turned completely around. I'm still married and using that book to help saved troubled marriages today.

Sometimes we don't want to take action, but when God says take action, we must do it. There is no time to waste wondering if we should take action or respond when the Lord has spoken. The same way we respond when God speaks audibly is the same way we should respond when He speaks to us in a dream or vision.

Dreams and visions are given to us so that we can move forward in our lives. Some people may get mad because they had a correcting dream. Correction dreams are not bad. They are God's way of telling us we need to be on a different path.

God wants to give great dreams and visions to the body of Christ. However, He is looking for those who will respond and make efforts toward change. Will you be the one to respond to when He speaks?

Conclusion

EMBRACE YOUR SEER GIFT

DEAR SEER, I pray that this book has been a guide to help you walk boldly in your seer gift. I pray that you have been given the peace you have been seeking and that your hunger for more has been reignited.

If you came to this book feeling beaten down by people, overlooked, rejected or scorned... If you have been told your dream gift doesn't mean anything, that it is of the devil, I pray that you have been encouraged and strengthened in God and in the unique way He has gifted you.

If I can leave you with anything, I want to say this: you are not strange. You are not crazy. You are having supernatural experiences with an awesome God.

I have been on a journey with the Holy Spirit, and it has taken me to the heights of His glory and the depths of His love that I never could have imagined. I am confident that God still speaks to us in dreams, that the seer gift is needed now more than ever, and that God never intended for this gift to become dormant among His people. He is looking for those who will be obedient to Him so that He can unlock this specific gift and calling in the lives of His people.

A significant portion of the Bible dedicated to this subject and if you think about how much time the average person spends sleeping throughout their lives, it is not hard to draw the conclusion that the dream realm is significant to our lives. If the average person lives about seventy-five years and they sleep about eight hours a night, then this means they would have slept approximately twenty-five years of their life. With all that time spent in the dream realm, how much revelation could one receive if they took their dream life seriously?

Scripture tells us in Joel 2:28 that "it shall come to pass afterward, that I will pour out my spirit upon all flesh; and your sons and your daughters shall prophesy, your old men shall dream dreams, your young men shall see visions" (KJV).

This is so true for today. The world is having visions and dreaming dreams. They are calling out for those who can interpret. The biggest issue is that they are turning to the world for the answers because the realm of darkness has embraced the supernatural and the body of Christ is just now catching up.

The Answer to a Desperate World

I remember one of the first times I overheard someone telling a dream and something clicked in me. For some reason, I knew what it meant. I have always been able to interpret or understand my own dreams. It wasn't really until that day that I realized I could understand other people's.

I was sitting on the steps at my childhood home, and I was listening to one of my mother's friends recount a dream she had that involved a roller coaster. What peaked my interest was the roller coaster? As I listened to her tell the dream, I thought to myself, "That's how she feels about her life, that it's out of control, up and down, and all over the place." Then I said what I was thinking to my mother. My mother relayed the message, and to my astonishment, she said I was exactly right.

Once word got out that I could in fact interpret dreams, it wasn't long before people were calling and asking me for understanding. This kind of excitement and urgency to understand dreams and visions continues today and is one of the hallmarks of my ministry to the body of Christ.

People are hungry for divine revelation. They are desperate to hear from God about who they are and what they are supposed to do with their lives on Earth. Prophets and seers have the advantage in this area to give people what they so desire. Being able to hear from God means the world for so many. His word brings life to dead places and light to dark places. We should count it a privilege that we have been given all the spiritual gifts and resources to bring a lost world back to God.

The seer's advantage is one that should no longer be underestimated or underutilized. There is a supernatural and eternal purpose in having this gift. This gift will position you for greatness. There are things that come with this gift when we walk this gift out the way we are supposed to.

Seer, I speak to you now in the name of Jesus, arise and take your place within the body of Christ. Don't shrink back, and don't fade into the background. Somebody is waiting for your unique insight. You are God's answer to somebody's problem. There is an advantage to your supernatural sight. It's called the seer's advantage!

Appendix A

REFERENCES TO DREAMS IN SCRIPTURE

OLD TESTAMENT

God used visions in the Old Testament to reveal His plan, to further His plan, and to put His people in places of influence.

- Abraham (Genesis 15:1): God used a vision to restate the Abrahamic Covenant, reminding Abram that he would have a son and be the father of many nations.

- Abimelech (Genesis 20:1–7): Abraham's wife, Sarah, was beautiful—so beautiful that when Abraham came into a new area he occasionally feared that the local ruler would kill him and take Sarah for himself. Abraham told Abimelech king of Gerar that Sarah was his sister (she was his half-sister). Abimelech took Sarah into his harem, but God sent him a dream telling him not to touch Sarah because she was Abraham's wife. The king returned Sarah to her husband the next morning; the dream had protected Sarah and safeguarded God's plan for Sarah to be the mother of His chosen people.

- Jacob (Genesis 28:10–17): Jacob, with his mother's help, stole Esau's firstborn inheritance. Jacob then fled Esau's anger, and on his journey, he had his famous dream of a ladder reaching to heaven on which angels ascended and descended. In this dream Jacob received God's promise that

Abraham's blessing would be carried on through him.

- Joseph (Genesis 37:1–11): Joseph is one of the most famous dreamers and dream interpreters in the Bible. His first recorded dreams are found in Genesis 37. They showed through easily deciphered symbols that Joseph's family would one day bow to him in respect. His brothers didn't appreciate the dream and, in their hatred, sold Joseph into slavery. Eventually, Joseph ended up in prison in Egypt.

- Pharaoh's cupbearer and baker (Genesis 40): While in prison Joseph interpreted some dreams of Pharaoh's cupbearer and baker. With God's guidance, he explained that the cupbearer would return to Pharaoh's service, but the baker would be killed.

- Pharaoh (Genesis 41): Two years later, Pharaoh himself had a dream which Joseph interpreted. God's purpose was to raise Joseph to second-in-command over Egypt and to save the Egyptians and the Israelites from a horrible famine.

- Samuel (1 Samuel 3): Samuel had his first vision as a young boy. God told him that judgment was coming upon the sons of Samuel's mentor, Eli. The young Samuel was faithful to relay the information, and God continued to speak to Samuel through the rest of his life.

- The Midianite and Amalekite armies (Judges 7:12–15): The pagan enemies of Israel had a divinely inspired dream. God told Gideon to sneak into the enemy camp at night, and there in the outposts of the camp, Gideon overheard an enemy soldier relate a dream he had just had. The interpretation, from another enemy soldier, mentioned Gideon by name and predicted that Israel would win the battle. Gideon was greatly encouraged by this revelation.

- Solomon (1 Kings 3:5): It was in a dream that God gave Solomon the famous offer: "Ask what you wish Me to give you." Solomon chose wisdom.

- Daniel (Daniel 2; 4): As He had done for Joseph, God placed Daniel in a position of power and influence by allowing him to interpret a foreign ruler's dream. This is consistent with God's propensity to use miracles to identify His messengers. Daniel himself had many dreams and visions, mostly related to future kingdoms of the world and the nation of Israel.

NEW TESTAMENT DREAMS AND VISIONS

Visions in the New Testament also served to provide information that was unavailable elsewhere. Specifically, God used visions and dreams to identify Jesus and to establish His church.

- Zacharias (Luke 1:5–23): God used a vision to tell Zacharias, an old priest, that he would soon have an important son. Not long after, Zacharias and his wife, Elizabeth, had John the Baptist.

- Joseph (Matthew 1:20; 2:13): Joseph would have divorced Mary when he found out she was pregnant, but God sent an angel to him in a dream, convincing him that the pregnancy was of God. Joseph went ahead with the marriage. After Jesus was born, God sent two more dreams: one to tell Joseph to take his family to Egypt so Herod could not kill

Jesus and another to tell him Herod was dead and that he could return home.

- Pilate's wife (Matthew 27:19): During Jesus's trial, Pilate's wife sent an urgent message to the governor encouraging him to free Jesus. Her message was prompted by a dream she had—a nightmare, really—that convinced her that Jesus was innocent, and that Pilate should have nothing to do with His case.

- Ananias (Acts 9:10): It would have taken nothing less than a vision from God to convince Ananias, a Christian in Damascus, to visit Paul, the persecutor of Christians. But because Ananias was obedient to God's leading, Paul regained his sight and found the truth about those he was trying to kill.

- Cornelius (Acts 10:1–6): God spoke to an Italian centurion named Cornelius who feared the God of the Jews. In his vision, Cornelius saw an angel who told him where to find Simon Peter and to send for him and listen to his message. Cornelius obeyed the vision, Peter came and preached, and Cornelius and his household full of Gentiles were saved by the grace of God.

- Peter (Acts 10:9–15): While Peter was praying on the rooftop of a house in Joppa, God gave him a vision of animals lowered in something like a sheet. A voice from heaven told Peter to kill the animals (some of which were unclean) and eat them. The vision served to show that Christians are not bound by kosher law and that God had pronounced Gentiles "clean"; that is, heaven is open to all who follow Jesus.

References to Dreams in Scripture

- Paul: Paul had several visions in his missionary career. One sent him to preach in Macedonia (Acts 16:9–10). Another encouraged him to keep preaching in Corinth (Acts 18:9–11). God also gave him a vision of heaven (2 Cor. 12:1–6).

- John (Revelation): Nearly the entire Book of Revelation is a vision John had while exiled on the island of Patmos. John's vision explains in more detail some of the events that God had shown Daniel.

Appendix B

SYMBOLIC NUMBERS AND COLORS IN DREAMS[1]

THE FOLLOWING DREAM symbols and their definitions are a compilation of my own experiences and thoughts as well as the works of Dr. Joe Ibojie, John Paul Jackson, James and Michal Ann Goll, and Sharnael Wolverton.

BASIC NUMBERS AND THEIR MEANINGS	
One	God/Godhead, beginning, source
Two	Multiplication, division or separation
Three	God/the Godhead, complete, the Holy Spirit
Four	Rule or dominion, creation or creative works
Five	Grace, abundance, favor
Six	Human, not of God, works
Seven	Divine perfection, rest spiritual completion
Eight	New beginnings, strength, worship
Nine	Finality and judgment, end, or conclusion
Ten	Complete, full
Eleven	Disorder, transition
Twelve	Perfect government or rule, apostolic fullness
Thirteen	Rebellion, sin or backsliding
Fourteen	Double measure of spiritual perfection, passover
Fifteen	Acts of divine grace, resurrection
Sixteen	Abomination, renewal of relationship with God

Seventeen	The perfection of spiritual order, walk with God
Eighteen	Judgment by the word, fruitful association
Nineteen	Complete judgment, fullness of spirit
Twenty	Expectancy, waiting, accountability

BASIC COLORS AND THEIR MEANINGS		
Color	**Positive Meaning**	**Negative Meaning**
Red	Wisdom, anointing power	Anger, war
White	Spirit of the Lord, holy power	Religious spirit
Yellow	Mind, hope, gift of God	Fear, coward, intellectual ascent
Silver	Redemption	Legalism, slavery, domination
Purple	Authority, royalty	False authority
Orange	Perseverance	Stubbornness, strong-willed
Pink	Emotions, love	Flesh, hate
Green	Conscience, growth, prosperity	Envy, jealousy, pride
Gold	Holy, purity, glory	Idolatry, defilement
Brown	Compassion, humility	Humanism
Blue	Communion, revelation	Depression, sorrow, anxiety
Black	Financially sound	Without the spirit

NOTES

INTRODUCTION
WELCOME TO THE DREAMER'S REALM CHAPTER ONE

1. BlueLetterBible.com, s.v. "*nabiy*," https://www.blueletterbible.org/lang/lexicon/lexicon.cfm?t=kjv&strongs=h5030.

CHAPTER ONE
WHAT MAKES THE SEER AND THE PROPHET DIFFERENT?

1. James Goll, *The Seer*, Expanded Edition (Shippensburg, PA: Destiny Image, 2012).
2. BlueLetterBible.org, s.v. "1 Chronicles 29:29," https://www.blueletterbible.org/kjv/1ch/29/29/t_conc_367029.
3. BlueLetterBible.org, s.v. "*ra'ah*," https://www.blueletterbible.org/lang/lexicon/lexicon.cfm?Strongs=H7200&t=KJV.
4. BlueLetterBible.org, s.v. "*chozeh*," https://www.blueletterbible.org/lang/lexicon/lexicon.cfm?Strongs=H2374&t=KJV.

CHAPTER TWO
CHARACTERISTICS OF THE SEER

1. Solid Rock Ministries, "Zachariah the Prophet," SolidRockLC.org, April 17, 2017, https://www.solidrocklc.org/sharons-eye-view/2017/4/17/day-6-zechariah-the-prophet.

CHAPTER FOUR
HOW THE SEER GIFT POSITIONS YOU

1. Charles John Ellicott, *A Bible Commentary for English Readers* (London: Cassell and Co., N.d.).

CHAPTER EIGHT
A PROPHET, NOT A PSYCHIC

1. BlueLetterBible.org, "The Canon of Scripture," https://www.blueletterbible.org/faq/canon.cfm.

CHAPTER NINE
REALMS OF THE SPIRIT

1. From *Easton's Bible Dictionary* as quoted on BibleGateway.com, s.v. "trance," https://www.biblegateway.com/resources/eastons-bible-dictionary/Trance.

2. Ibid.

APPENDIX

1. Data in this appendix was compiled and re-presented from my own experiences and thoughts as well as from the following sources: Joe Ibojie, *Illustrated Dictionary of Dream Symbols* (Shippensburg, PA: Destiny Image, 2010); John Paul Jackson, *Understanding Dreams and Visions*, Course 201 (N.p.: Stream Music Group, 2003); James W. and Michal Ann Goll, *Dream Language* (Shippensburg, PA: Destiny Image, 2006); Sharnael Wolverton, *Seers Handbook* (Denham Springs, LA: Swiftfire Publishing, 2007).

Made in the USA
Coppell, TX
12 October 2022